Why Did Jesus Die

and What Difference Does It Make?

THE JESUS WAY
—SMALL BOOKS *of* RADICAL FAITH—

Why Did Jesus Die

and What Difference Does It Make?

MICHELE HERSHBERGER

Harrisonburg, Virginia

Herald Press
PO Box 866, Harrisonburg, Virginia 22803
www.HeraldPress.com

Library of Congress Cataloging-in-Publication Data
Names: Hershberger, Michele, 1960- author.
Title: Why did Jesus die and what difference does it make? / Michele Hershberger.
Description: Harrisonburg : Herald Press, 2019. | Series: The Jesus way series | Includes bibliographical references. | Summary: "Why did Jesus die? And how does his death change us and our world? The author delves into the meaning of the cross by sifting through Scripture and the life of Christ; teaches theological concepts like sin, salvation, and atonement. Accessible Jesus-centered theology from an Anabaptist perspective"-- Provided by publisher.
Identifiers: LCCN 2019023919 | ISBN 9781513805658 (paperback) | ISBN 9781513806136 (ebook)
Subjects: LCSH: Atonement. | Jesus Christ--Crucifixion.
Classification: LCC BT265.3 .H47 2019 | DDC 232/.3--dc23
LC record available at https://lccn.loc.gov/2019023919

WHY DID JESUS DIE AND WHAT DIFFERENCE DOES IT MAKE?
© 2019 by Herald Press, Harrisonburg, Virginia 22803. 800-245-7894.
   All rights reserved.
Library of Congress Control Number: 2019023919
International Standard Book Number: 978-1-5138-0565-8 (paperback);
   978-1-5138-0613-6 (ebook)
Printed in United States of America
Cover and interior design by Reuben Graham

All rights reserved. This publication may not be reproduced, stored in a retrieval system, or transmitted in whole or in part, in any form, by any means, electronic, mechanical, photocopying, recording or otherwise without prior permission of the copyright owners.

Unless otherwise noted, Scripture text is quoted, with permission, from the *New Revised Standard Version*, © 1989, Division of Christian Education of the National Council of Churches of Christ in the United States of America.

23 22 21 20 19   10 9 8 7 6 5 4 3 2 1

Contents

Introduction to The Jesus Way Series from Herald Press 7
Introduction 9

1 How Does Jesus Save Us—and from What? 13
2 What Does Jesus Say about Atonement? 23
3 What Does Paul Say about Atonement? 37
4 What Does the Church Say about Atonement? 53
5 How Does Atonement Transform Us? 71

Glossary 81
Discussion and Reflection Questions 85
Shared Convictions 89
Notes 91
The Author 95

Introduction to The Jesus Way Series from Herald Press

The Jesus Way is good news for all people, of all times, in all places. Jesus Christ "is before all things, and in him all things hold together"; "in him all the fullness of God was pleased to dwell" (Colossians 1:17, 19). The Jesus Way happens when God's will is done on earth as it is in heaven.

But what does it mean to walk the Jesus Way? How can we who claim the name of Christ reflect the image of God in the twenty-first century? What does it mean to live out and proclaim the good news of reconciliation in Christ?

The Jesus Way: Small Books of Radical Faith offers concise, practical theology that helps readers encounter big questions about God's work in the world. Grounded in a Christ-centered reading of Scripture and a commitment to reconciliation, the series aims to enliven the service and embolden the witness of people who follow Jesus. The volumes in the series are written by a diverse community of internationally renowned pastors, scholars, and practitioners committed to the way of Jesus.

The Jesus Way series is rooted in Anabaptism, a Christian tradition that prioritizes following Jesus, loving enemies, and creating faithful communities. During the Protestant Reformation of the 1500s, early Anabaptists who began meeting for worship emphasized discipleship in addition to belief, baptized adults instead of infants, and pledged their allegiance to God over loyalty to the state. Early Anabaptists were martyred for their radical faith, and they went to their deaths without violently resisting their accusers.

Today more than two million Anabaptist Christians worship in more than one hundred countries around the globe. They include Mennonites, Amish, Brethren in Christ, and Hutterites. Many other Christians committed to Anabaptist beliefs and practices remain in church communities in other traditions.

Following Jesus means turning from sin, renouncing violence, seeking justice, believing in the reconciling power of God, and living in the power of the Holy Spirit. The Jesus Way liberates us from conformity to the world and heals broken places. It shines light on evil and restores all things.

Join Christ-followers around the world as we seek the Jesus Way.

Introduction

Walking home from work one day, I saw a bright pink piece of paper stuck between my front door and the trim. It looked like a little flag, a sign of hope waiting for me on my front porch. Maybe it was a flyer for a neighbor's party, or a sale bill, or a note from a friend?

As I walked onto my front porch, I saw that it was a gospel tract. The idea that someone had tucked into my door a message about Jesus, the cross, and my eternal destination filled me with mixed emotions. On one hand, I'm glad that people care enough about me to walk onto my front porch to share with me something about God. On the other hand, can eight tiny pages, complete with graphics and four to five Bible verses, sum up what it means to be a Christian? It seems inadequate. The Bible can seem overwhelming to the new reader, but can a tract sum up the work of Jesus?

What is God like, according to this tract? The pink pages showed a big cross that bridged sinful humanity and a holy

God. Somehow the death of Jesus created the only way for me to get to God. "Jesus died on the cross to save us from our sins," the booklet said. As a Christian and a Bible professor, I agree with that statement. The question remains, How?

If a tract and a warm conversation can help people find a church community and begin a relationship with Jesus, then I'm supportive of these efforts in every way. But what if those who left that tract on my porch were asking only one of many questions? What if there are other pressing issues besides my eternal destiny? What if Jesus wants more than my accepting him as my personal Savior?

The tract on my porch was about getting saved. While this book is not about salvation per se, salvation is connected to Jesus and his work, particularly what happened when Jesus died on the cross. And that question—What is the meaning of the work of Christ?—*is* the topic of this book. We call the work of Christ *atonement*, and many times we answer this question in ways that involve both the cross and "getting saved." **Atonement** comes from the term *at-one-ment*, or the reality of being one with God. Atonement theories seek to describe what this reality means and how we achieve it. Views of the atonement seek to give biblical reasons why Jesus was crucified on a cross, how the rest of the life of Jesus is connected to that event, and what all this says about who God is.

The central question of this book is, What does the death of Jesus mean, and how does that death affect individuals, communities, and the whole cosmos? This question is of utmost importance. We long to become one with God, and we struggle to understand how Jesus being executed by Roman authorities more than two thousand years ago helps us do that.

Our view of the atonement functions like a stone skipped on the water; it has ripple effects over the entire theological pond. So it's important to ask many questions and delve deeply into Scripture. What is the character of God? Is the character of God consistent with the life, teachings, death, and resurrection of Jesus? Why did Jesus come to earth? Is there saving importance to the life, teachings, and miracles of Jesus? How does the cross work to save us? What does it mean to be saved? How does atonement work at a corporate level as well as with individuals? How is the cross part of God's intention for the whole cosmos? How does our view on atonement influence our sense of right and wrong? How do the various scriptural explanations for the death of Jesus work together?

These are the questions we'll struggle with in this book. Our goal is to understand atonement in its original context as best we can. Key terms appear in bold and are defined in the glossary. In chapter 1, we'll look at the truth that Jesus saves us and heals us. In chapter 2, we will look at how Jesus talked about the purpose of his life and death. In chapter 3, we will look at what the apostle Paul said about the atonement. In chapter 4, we'll look at how the early church interpreted the work of Christ to reunite us with God, and how that understanding changed throughout church history. In chapter 5, we'll evaluate, as best we can, what the atonement means for us.

This is a humble journey, because atonement is complicated. But when we invite God into our ponderings, and when we search the Scriptures together, we can trust God to help us understand.

Gospel tracts on front porches can point us to good news, because they can be the beginning of a beautiful, life-changing journey with Jesus. Discerning how the death—and life—of Jesus makes this journey possible is the theological endeavor of this book.

Join me on the porch.

1

How Does Jesus Save Us—and from What?

Once there were two families who lived with alcoholism. In both families, one member got drunk every Friday night, came home, and verbally abused and sometimes beat the other members of his or her family. Both were terrible situations of fear and bondage.

The first family reacted to the person who was alcoholic in this way: every Saturday morning, after the drunken brawl and the abuse, they forgave her. They loved her, and they listened to her pleas for forgiveness and accepted them. But the next Friday night, she would go out and get drunk again. When she was put in jail, the family would pay the bond. The pattern stayed the same, week after week after week.

The second family also loved their family member who was alcoholic. And they also forgave him. But one Saturday morning, they decided to open the way for him to get sober. They offered to get him into a treatment center, where he could get help. He got sober; he found healing. Before he was addicted and in bondage to this habit, and now he was free. He didn't drink anymore. He was not only forgiven; he was set free.

The first family offered forgiveness. The second family offered forgiveness *and* healing. We could say that the second family gave their loved one a fuller *salvation* than the first family.

What do these stories have to do with atonement? Like the second family, Jesus longs to provide real deliverance from whatever holds us in bondage. Atonement is our word for the *how* of that deliverance: how Jesus both saves us and heals us.

How can we again become "at one" with God? Why did Jesus have to die, and how does this death save us? How is the death of Jesus different from the death of another noble person, like Martin Luther King Jr.?

Although it's more complicated than the stories of the loved ones with alcoholism would suggest, the atonement means that Jesus came not only to forgive us or pay the bond to get us out of jail; he also made a way for us to "get sober" from our addictions, our ways of harming ourselves and others, our sins. As we will see, this atonement comes to us not only by his death. Jesus also saves us by his birth, life, teachings, and resurrection. In that way, it's better to define atonement not just as what happened on the cross but, more broadly, as the work of Christ.

WHY IS ATONEMENT NECESSARY?

What makes atonement necessary? The Bible gives us a one-word answer: sin. Yet we shouldn't be fooled into thinking that this one word—sin—is a simple, one-dimensional concept. It isn't. The Bible uses many words that hover around the

1. How Does Jesus Save Us—and from What?   15

general theme of sin. Adding to that complexity is the fact that different cultures understand the concept of sin with different shades of meaning; we need to honor this reality. Yet we can also get a foundational grounding in what sin means by looking at four stories in Genesis.

Genesis 3–11 offers us four narratives that show the danger of sin. The stories of Adam and Eve, Cain and Abel, the flood, and the Tower of Babel show us how sin breaks four major relationships in our lives. Take the Adam and Eve narrative. They disobey God by eating the forbidden fruit. This breaks their relationship with *God*. Adam and Eve blame each other, thus illustrating how sin breaks our relationship with other *people*. In their lostness, they realize they're naked. This symbolizes shame, or a broken relationship we experience in our inner *self* when we sin. Finally, the ground is cursed, and childbearing becomes unbearable. Sin also destroys our relationship with the physical *world*.

God, of course, responds. Adam and Eve are sent out of the garden. And while this feels like a terrible judgment, it's also grace. God doesn't want them to eat fruit from the second tree, the tree of eternal life, because this would then leave them in a sinful state forever. It's a paradox: God, in mercy, gives them judgment. It's also important to note that God doesn't withdraw from them. After Adam and Eve sin, Yahweh walks in the garden, calling out, "Where are you?" (Genesis 3:9). God is right there, up close and personal with sinful humanity. This is important to remember when we encounter views of atonement that emphasize a God who withdraws, or a God who is not able to handle our sin, or a God who does not want to be close to us.

In the other three stories from Genesis—Cain and Abel, the flood, and the Tower of Babel—the same four relationships are broken through sin: with God, with others, with self, and with the natural world. If sin is the problem, then salvation is the solution. Atonement is the *how* of salvation. If sin breaks these four relationships, then salvation, however we might understand it, needs to heal these same four relationships. And Jesus is all about healing.

JESUS HEALS BROKEN RELATIONSHIPS

Jesus cares deeply about our broken relationship with God. The cross brings this healing, and the rest of the book will center on what that means. Yet Jesus also healed this relationship *before* his death. He forgave people's sins before he ever died on the cross (Mark 2:1-12). Without eliminating the connection between forgiveness and the cross, we must admit that it was possible for Jesus—and God—to forgive sins without this "payment." The four Gospels are filled with stories of Jesus working to heal our brokenness with God. In the story of the prodigal son, Jesus shows us who God is by describing a forgiving father who bends over backward to welcome home a wayward child. John 3:16 says that it was for love that God sent Jesus into the world.

Jesus also healed the broken relationships that people experience with each other. His birth to poor peasants, instead of to a priestly family, showed God's heart for the poor. Jesus taught us to love our enemies, and he did so himself. First-century Jews had to realign their belief that sick people were terrible sinners, because Jesus healed those unclean people. Jesus forgave the soldiers who crucified him, for they did not know what they were doing (Luke 23:34).

Jesus knew the pain of inner shame—of separation from the self—and worked to heal it. While many of his healings were private, and while he sometimes asked those he healed not to tell anyone, Jesus went public with the healing when that healing couldn't be visibly ratified. He knew that diseased persons suffered not only from physical disease but also from being social outcasts. He wanted to heal that broken relationship too (see Luke 8:40-56).

Finally, Jesus cared about the physical world. He didn't just forgive sins, important as that is; he didn't just teach in such a way that the law was fulfilled (Matthew 5:17). He cared about physical needs. He fed thousands of people. He healed people who were blind and those who were paralyzed. And he challenged unjust realities like the temple system, which made people so poor that they couldn't care for themselves or their families. He condemned the religious leaders for adding to the burden of the poor. He even overcame creation's worst enemy—death. God resurrected Jesus, bringing his dead body back to life. In this mighty event, God gave a hearty yes to the goodness of the physical world.

These four broken relationships continue to be healed by the Holy Spirit, who moves among us. The Spirit comforts us, challenges us, convicts us of sin, and guides us in our discipleship.

THE RESULTS OF SIN

Ask most Christians to define sin, and they'll talk about disobeying God or neglecting to do what God has called us to do. But ask people about the *results* of sin, and you get different answers. Many emphasize how sin damages our relationship with God. Only a few give attention to how sin hurts the relationships we have with others, the physical world, and our own selves. But sin works like a wrecking ball against those relationships too.

If we view the results of sin too narrowly, then we view atonement too narrowly, and we limp through life. Our sins may be forgiven, but our lives are not fully restored. This is not to say that our relationship with God isn't important; it is paramount. But God longs for us to have full salvation—full "at-one-ment." If our view of the atonement doesn't include a way for all these relationships to be healed, then we have a weak salvation. If our view of the atonement gets our sins forgiven but leaves us stuck in brokenness, unable to love our enemies or even love ourselves, then our salvation is incomplete. It leaves us captive to our addictions, in much the same way that the person with alcoholism in the first family was forgiven but still stuck. Jesus wants to heal not only our relationship with God but the other broken relationships too. Yes, Jesus brought salvation through his death, but also through his life, teaching, miracles, and resurrection, and through the gift of the Holy Spirit.

Why is a fuller definition of sin important? It's not only in the first four "fall stories" of Genesis that we see the wrecking-ball effect of sin; it's everywhere in the Bible. People hurt each other—think Jacob and Esau. People stumble with the weight of their guilt—think David after his affair with Bathsheba. And sin hurts God's beautiful creation—we see that "the whole creation has been groaning" (Romans 8:22) and that people with diseased bodies are pleading with Jesus for healing.

Our view of atonement must take into account all of Jesus' life. This truth remains a paradox. For while it's true that Jesus was saving people before he died on the cross, it's also true that the *death* of Jesus is key to our becoming one with God.

HOW WE SEE JESUS AND WHY IT MATTERS

Our view of atonement influences how we see Jesus and what it means to follow him. If we have a narrow view, then we believe that Jesus came to die for only one reason—to pay for our sins, in whatever way we interpret that metaphor. But it's equally true to say that Jesus was killed. When we say it that way, everything changes. Yes, Jesus died on the cross for our sins. And yes, he was executed by agents of the state.

We could say that Jesus died for spiritual reasons and was killed for historical ones. The truth of the first statement doesn't contradict the truth of the second. The Romans sought to get rid of Jesus because he was a threat. He was collecting a following, and they had seen other messiahs do the same thing, with violent uprisings as a result. They didn't want that kind of trouble. When Jesus rode into the city on a donkey, his people hailed him as a king, and that didn't sit well with authorities either. As Messiah, Jesus saw his purpose as setting people free (Luke 4:16-19); he had to challenge oppression and injustice. And those in power hate to be challenged. If Jesus was going to speak out for justice and commit to being nonviolent all the way to the cross, it's easy to see why he got killed.

But it wasn't just the Romans who wanted Jesus dead. The Jewish religious leaders likewise were threatened. Jesus healed on the Sabbath, clearly against their understanding of Mosaic Law. He challenged their theological claims, and the common people loved him for it. He called the Pharisees a "brood of vipers" (Matthew 12:34), and that wasn't exactly complimentary either. The religious leaders hated him so much that they gave up their most cherished belief—that Yahweh was the only King—to ensure that Pilate would go through with the crucifixion. They said, "We have no king but the emperor" (John 19:15). They had no warm feelings toward Caesar, but they were willing to call him king if it meant getting rid of Jesus.

Jesus died for our sins. Jesus was killed for being a threat to oppressive systems. We can believe both to be true. In fact, without this balance, we don't fully understand atonement. If Jesus *only* died for our sins, then his death on the cross carries only one meaning for us—that through the cross we get saved. This is a wonderful and important part of why he died, but it's crucial to see that Jesus was also killed because he challenged unjust structures and systems. At the same time, if Jesus *only* died because he was a threat to the state, he is just one more in a long line of courageous people who stood up to oppression and, by so doing, got themselves killed. We need to be saved from both personal sin and unjust systems, not just from one or the other.

TAKE UP YOUR CROSS

Jesus told his disciples—and us—that all who want to follow him must "deny themselves and take up their cross daily and follow me" (Luke 9:23). He said these words before he hung on a cross himself. So the cross must symbolize something in addition to the way he paid for our sins. Why? Because if you and I are called to carry our crosses, it must be for a purpose other than dying for the sins of others. We aren't Jesus.

To carry our cross is to be ready to suffer for following Jesus. "For those who want to save their life will lose it, and those who lose their life for my sake will save it," Jesus said. "What does it profit them if they gain the whole world, but lose or forfeit themselves?" (Luke 9:24-25). Like Jesus, we are called to nonviolently challenge the evil structures of our world and to remain nonviolent in the face of death. If we do both things—challenge evil and refuse to defend ourselves—it's clear we'll suffer. And this daring discipleship gives us "the whole world."

Somehow, in the mystery of Jesus, when we lose ourselves for the sake of the kingdom, we gain. We save our lives when we lose them. There is danger in emphasizing discipleship to the degree that we try to follow Jesus out of our own willpower. Yet it's also true that we will only be fulfilled when we pour out our very lives to Jesus, not to earn our favor with God but as a natural response to the deliverance Jesus gave us.

Carrying our cross is what discipleship, or following Jesus, is all about. It's a calling for every Christian, not just some of us.[1]

How we understand the saving significance of the cross also influences how we understand our lives as Christians. Are we only forgiven, or can we be transformed? Who does the transforming? Does the cross work *for* us, as in on our behalf, or does it work *inside* us? Or both? Is accepting Jesus as Lord and Savior the end of the journey or the starting point? Is getting saved the same thing as being healed? How can we be disciples and do good works not to earn God's favor but out of gratitude for being healed?

These questions matter. How we answer them determines whether we are more like the first family at the opening of this chapter or the second. How we answer them determines what our lives as followers of Jesus look like.

2

What Does Jesus Say about Atonement?

You would think that, after walking with Jesus and living with him 24/7, the disciples would have had an atonement theory all worked out. They didn't. Not only were they unsure about *why* Jesus died, they didn't even expect that he would—at least not death by Roman execution. Peter, James, and John slept while Jesus prayed in agony. Peter reacted violently to the soldiers coming to arrest Jesus at Gethsemane. When times got tough, they all ran—except Peter. And while he showed courage in sticking close to the trial scene, Peter also did the one thing he swore he'd never do: deny Jesus. The crucifixion came as a shock.

And it wasn't any easier after his death. Cleopas and his friend, both disciples of Jesus, walked from Jerusalem to Emmaus with their heads bowed in sorrow. The one they thought would be the Messiah had been killed (Luke 24:18-21).

For them and the others, the concept of the Messiah did not match up with a humiliating crucifixion. It didn't make sense.

What we today may think is obvious about the atonement was not apparent to the little band of disciples. Their confusion is proof that Jesus' death did not neatly fit into their expectations. There was something about Jesus' death they didn't really want to hear, which may also be true for us today. This is not to say that Jesus didn't fulfill the prophecies of old, which he revealed to those on the road to Emmaus (see Luke 24:26-27); it's just that the way in which he fulfilled those prophecies wasn't immediately apparent.

As we discussed, atonement is the work of Christ to bring us into union with God, self, others, and creation. Jesus' death on the cross is a key component of his work. Yet the cross is not the only way Jesus saves and heals us; Jesus' life, teachings, miracles, resurrection and the coming of the Holy Spirit all work together to heal the four relationships that sin disrupts. We also noted the historical reasons that Jesus was killed, as well as the fact that these reasons—essentially, that Jesus threatened the powers that be—are important for us to remember. If we are to follow Jesus, then challenging injustice is part of our job too.

But the questions still haunt us. How does the cross save us? Thousands of people were crucified by the Romans in first-century Palestine. Why was this death different? The best way to answer this question is to start with Jesus himself.

JESUS AS THE SUFFERING SERVANT

Before we look at the specific words Jesus used to explain his death, it's important to hear what Jesus believed to be his mission. The clearest purpose statement Jesus made is found in Luke 4:16-21, where Jesus came back to his hometown of

Nazareth as the guest Torah reader. He was given the scroll of Isaiah, where he read verses 1-2 of chapter 61. After reading, Jesus said, "Today this scripture has been fulfilled in your hearing" (Luke 4:21).

This announcement sent ripples over the congregation. Isaiah 61:1-2 includes the word *anointed*, which in Hebrew is also the origin of the word *Messiah*. Jesus, the hometown boy, was claiming to be the Messiah! And he was doing so in the context of one of Isaiah's suffering servant songs. This illuminated what kind of Messiah he would be.

Let's look at the prophet Isaiah's words more closely. Isaiah proclaimed the news of a coming suffering servant in five key passages: Isaiah 42:1-4; 49:1-7; 50:4-9; 52:13–53:12; and 61:1-2. It's possible that in Isaiah's mind, the servant was Israel, a righteous remnant of Israel, or even the prophet himself. Yet certain parts of these passages in Isaiah—what we call the Servant Songs or "songs of the suffering servant"—point toward a single person, one commissioned by God. By the first century, Jews interpreted these songs as prophecies of the Messiah. But the rabbis debated whether the suffering fell on the Messiah, on Israel itself, or on the Gentiles. If the Messiah was to be sent directly from God and rule over the people, wouldn't he triumph over the Romans?

The life of Jesus echoes every Servant Song. In Isaiah 42:1-4, the chosen One will bring forth justice, but he will do so in a nonviolent way. This faithful One will be persistent even though it may look as if he's unsuccessful. In Isaiah 49:1-7, the suffering servant is called to be the light to the Gentiles. He is deeply despised but eventually exalted. In Isaiah 50:4-9, the suffering servant doesn't back down even in the midst of great suffering.

Isaiah 52:13–53:12 is especially important for our understanding of Jesus. Here the servant experiences profound humiliation and suffering. The suffering is vicarious; the servant suffers for others. He is the sin-bearer. And paradoxically, his immense suffering and execution, during which he remains nonviolent, brings restoration for all. His suffering is redemptive. This is the way of salvation. Finally, in Isaiah 61:1-4, the passage Jesus read a portion of in the Nazareth synagogue, the suffering servant will bring good news to the oppressed; proclaim Jubilee, or economic relief; and bring vengeance to the other nations.

In summary, the Servant Songs of Isaiah tell us these things: The suffering one is an agent to the nations. He is called to bring justice to all. He has been anointed—*Messiah*-ed—by the Spirit, and with the Spirit's power he is able to remain nonviolent. He faces unfathomable humiliation, opposition, and eventually a cruel death, all of which he accepts. At first it looks like he fails. In that sense, the suffering one only achieves his purpose because Yahweh intervenes. Seeing all this, the kings of the world confess and give up their rebellion. The nations are healed.

Back to the Nazareth synagogue. The interpretation Jesus gave to Isaiah 61 almost got him killed. It wasn't that the Nazareth crowd didn't want to hear this Scripture, which was about God's Jubilee, the "year of the Lord's favor," a time when they would find Sabbath rest in all areas of life, including economic freedom (Luke 4:19). And it wasn't that the congregation didn't want a messiah to deliver them, or even that they were specifically opposed to Jesus being the Messiah—although they did have their doubts, given that he was just the hometown boy.

The real rub was that Jesus didn't read all of Isaiah 61:1-2. He left out the part about the "day of vengeance of our God," a vengeance believed to be reserved for the Gentiles. Again, knowing their inner thoughts, Jesus reminded the congregation of two times that God's prophets showed Jubilee to Gentiles. Elijah rescued the widow of Zarephath, a widow in enemy Phoenicia. Elisha brought healing to the leper Naaman, a Syrian military captain. Hearing this, the crowd went wild with anger. Jubilee was meant for the Jews only, and this imposter messiah had to be destroyed. They led him to the cliff to throw him off, but somehow Jesus walked through the crowd and escaped.

The second time Jesus drew heavily from the suffering servant passages in Isaiah was in the hours between the Last Supper and his arrest, when the disciples were arguing over who would be the greatest. Peter declared he was ready to die for Jesus. Jesus told Peter that before the cock crowed, he would deny Jesus three times. Then he tried to explain to the disciples that difficult times were ahead. In the past, they visited towns without purse or sandals, lacking nothing. Now, said Jesus, they were to take purses along and buy a sword, even if it meant selling their cloaks. Then, in Luke 22:37, he quoted Isaiah 53:12: "Therefore I will allot him a portion with the great, and he shall divide the spoil with the strong; because he poured out himself to death, and *was numbered with the transgressors*; yet he bore the sin of many, and made intercession for the transgressors" (emphasis mine).

This verse would have called to mind the entire song, including the vicarious suffering of the servant and his intentional nonviolence. But the disciples forgot that part. Thinking he literally wanted them to have swords, they came up with two. In the Greek, Jesus' words sound scolding; while his words are often translated into English as "It is enough," they could just as easily be rendered "Enough of you!" or "Don't be foolish!" (Luke 22:38, my translation).

These two stories tell us much about Jesus and how he saw himself as the suffering servant. Like Isaiah's servant, Jesus saw his mission as one to all people. At the Nazareth synagogue, he was challenging ethnocentrism. His people were to be a light to the Gentiles, and they weren't being that. He longed to bring justice not only for the Jewish people but for all. And that justice encompassed a Jubilee-like release from both physical bondage and spiritual bondage. Jesus would go on from Nazareth doing exactly what he said he would do. He did bring physical and spiritual healing. He did bring good news to the oppressed. He did bind up the brokenhearted. And as the Luke 22:33-39 passage shows, Jesus also saw himself as the one called to vicariously suffer for the sake of all.

Other sayings and stories of Jesus point back to the Servant Songs as well. At Jesus' baptism, the voice from heaven quoted Isaiah 42:1, "with you I am well-pleased," singling him out as the Messiah (Matthew 3:13-17; Mark 1:9-11; Luke 3:21-22). In Mark 10:45, Jesus said, "For the Son of Man came not to be served but to serve, and to give his life a ransom for many." Both the words *serve* and *many* allude to the Servant Songs. In Isaiah 52:13–53:12, *many* is used four times. The original audience would have heard echoes here of this famous song.

Mark 10:45 offers another window into Jesus' understanding of his life and death. He saw himself as a *ransom*. There are several ways to interpret this word. In a world in which slaves were bought and sold, ransom could have meant the means by which a slave was set free, usually with a sum of money. Ransom also developed a meaning close to that of **propitiation**, or a payment to appease an angry God. As John Driver notes, in later Jewish thought, from the time of the Maccabees forward, the suffering of the righteous ones comes to have a propitiatory value. According to one source, the

2. What Does Jesus Say about Atonement?

Maccabees, Jewish rebel fighters, understood their martyrdom as "a ransom for our nation's sins, and through the blood of these righteous ones and their propitiating death, the divine Providence preserved Israel which before was evil entreated."[1] Like Jesus, the Maccabees were a "ransom for many," but for a different reason: they thought God was wrathful. Jesus was a ransom too, but there is no hint that the ransom was to God or that God needed or wanted it. We know from history that the Maccabees would become oppressors themselves. Jesus, with a different view of ransom, fought oppression without participating in it himself.

So what did Jesus mean when he said he came to "give his life a ransom for many"? In Mark 10, James and John were concerned with their status and asked Jesus if he would grant that the two of them receive a seat at his right and left hand, seats of the greatest honor. The brothers were mirroring the society around them, for they lived in a world in which status was the most important thing. In the Roman **patron-client system**, most people had those below them—the clients—and also people above them—the patrons. Patrons gave favors to their clients, and in turn, clients honored their patrons and publicly praised them. Everyone participated, and the ladder of status extended even to the emperor, who was the patron of all people but client to the gods.

Against this backdrop came Jesus' words: "For the Son of Man came not to be served but to serve, and to give his life a ransom for many." Jesus flipped the script, going against the patron-client system and opposing the Roman status system at its most fundamental level. And it is within this new worldview that we must contemplate Jesus' statement about his death.

Ransom means "release," or a method of release. The release could happen through a money transaction, in which a benefactor paid a price—a ransom—and then the slave was set free. But it could just as easily be a connection to the "ransom" God made to set the slaves free in Egypt. At the Red Sea, Yahweh ransomed Israel from their cruel Egyptian taskmasters. This was both a physical and spiritual deliverance: physical, as the Israelites were saved from backbreaking slavery and near starvation, and also spiritual, as Yahweh worked to set them spiritually free in the wilderness. In this historical echo, note that God redeemed Israel not by paying anyone off but by delivering the entire group. When Jesus called himself a "ransom for many," it's likely he meant he was setting humanity free, and he was doing so by being the servant of the Isaiah songs. And like the exodus-Sinai event, he was bringing humanity both spiritual deliverance and physical release from the bonds of oppression and status-seeking.

At the Nazareth synagogue, Jesus claimed the suffering servant identity as the one who would release captives and bring good news to the poor. But the question remains: How does Jesus, as the suffering servant, set us free and bring atonement? The writer of 1 Peter fills in the details. First Peter 2:22-25 quotes and reshapes Isaiah 53, with Jesus as the centerpiece. Here is the passage from 1 Peter (in regular type), with sections of Isaiah 53 inserted (in italics):

> "He committed no sin, and no deceit was found in his mouth." When he was abused, he did not return abuse; when he suffered, he did not threaten; but he entrusted himself to the one who judges justly. *He was oppressed, and he was afflicted, yet he did not open his mouth; like a lamb that is led to the slaughter, and like a sheep that before its shearers is silent, so he did not open his mouth* [Isaiah 53:7]. He himself bore our sins in his body on the cross, *borne our infirmities* [v. 4], so that, free from sins, we might live for righteousness; by his wounds you have

been healed *and by his bruises we are healed* [v. 5]. For you were going astray like sheep, but now you have returned to the shepherd and guardian of your souls. *All we like sheep have gone astray; we have all turned to our own way, and the* LORD *has laid on him the iniquity of us all* [v. 6].

According to 1 Peter, Jesus, the lamb and the servant, bore our sins—our infirmities—on the cross. This frees us from sin. In this way, there is a sacrifice. The sinless Jesus takes upon himself the sins of all of us, and we are set free. We've been healed by his wounds. Jesus is also the servant, and here we are reminded of his life and his upending of all power-grabbing, an addiction that surely enslaves all who participate. We have been set free, and the fruit of this freedom is our ability to "live for righteousness" (1 Peter 2:24).

Note what is not said and what is. Jesus' ransom, or rescue, can be both personal and corporate. Jesus on the cross heals us, bears our sins, and vicariously suffers in our place. We can use the metaphor without assuming there was a literal payment to anyone and without assuming that God needed Jesus to suffer in order to placate his anger. Sin breaks our relationship with God; Jesus' death, as well as the rest of his life, heals that relationship.

And this healing reaches not just "up" to God but outward, to every relationship. The servant identity of Jesus speaks a word against power-grabbing, status-seeking societies, such as the ancient Roman society and our world today. It's telling that all of Jesus' predictions of his upcoming death and resurrection come within narrative contexts of the disciples squabbling about who would be the greatest (Mark 8:31-33; 9:30-37; 10:32-41). Living in a culture in which status was highly valued, the disciples could hardly resist joining in the power grab. It was difficult to imagine a suffering servant

Messiah. If the disciples struggled to imagine Jesus as the suffering servant, it makes sense that we may have difficulty understanding atonement in this way as well.

JESUS AS THE PASSOVER LAMB

Jesus also spoke explicitly about the meaning of his death at the Last Supper. Here Jesus took his cues from the exodus out of Egypt, comparing himself to the Passover lamb. Just as a perfect lamb was sacrificed as part of God's deliverance of the slaves, so too Jesus would soon accomplish redemption from slavery—sin and other forms of bondage—with his own shed blood. In Egypt, God rescued an ethnically mixed group of slaves—anyone willing to put the blood of the lamb on their doorpost. Now Jesus would die to set the whole world free.

At the Last Supper, Jesus and the disciples were remembering the old covenant, reenacting God's rescue from slavery in Egypt by eating the Passover lamb. But Jesus was also inaugurating a new covenant by connecting the bread and wine to his body and blood. **Covenant** was a precious word for the Jewish people. It spoke of a relationship that encompassed all of life: ethics, worship rituals, how the people lived with their God. This formal but personal relationship is a concrete way to understand being "at one" with God. In covenant relationship with humans, God was always the initiator. God and the people fulfilled their part in this relational dance, and even when the people broke covenant in the Old Testament, a common occurrence, God was still faithful, showing steadfast, or covenant, love—***chesed*** in Hebrew. Many times God could have walked away when the people broke covenant, but God didn't.

It's clear that the New Testament writers took atonement cues from the Passover lamb metaphor. John the Baptist said

2. What Does Jesus Say about Atonement?

of Jesus, "Here is the Lamb of God who takes away the sins of the world!" (John 1:29). John's gospel also has Jesus crucified at the exact time that the Passover lambs were being slaughtered at the temple (John 19:14). John 19:36, describing Jesus' death on the cross, alludes to a rule about the Passover lamb: "You shall not break any of its bones" (Exodus 12:46). And when Jesus said, "Eat my flesh and drink my blood," in John 6:48-58, he was harking back to the Passover lamb. These were the words used in the sacred communal meal. These were words spoken in preparation for deliverance from slavery.

Today, some Christians have given these words the added meaning of **expiation**—being cleansed from sin—given by a priest. But being cleansed from sin has a different nuance than being rescued from slavery. Humans need both actions, and we do well to include all the context of the meaning of the word *lamb*, both as it is expressed in the Passover ritual and as it is articulated in the Day of Atonement ritual.

Lamb imagery appears again in Revelation, where the writer uses the term *lamb* thirty times as the central and defining metaphor for Jesus. Revelation 5:9-10 says, "You are worthy to take the scroll and to open its seals, for you were slaughtered and by your blood you ransomed for God saints from every tribe and language and people and nation; you have made them to be a kingdom and priests serving our God, and they will reign on earth." This Lamb of Revelation 5 is first called a Lion (v. 5), which would suggest one who conquers. John hears the word *Lion*, but he looks and sees a Lamb—and not just any lamb, but one who is slaughtered (the cross) and is standing (the resurrection).

Jesus is the Lion—that is, the one who conquers evil. And he is the Lion precisely because he is the Lamb: the one who vicariously and nonviolently suffers for others, even to death.

Surely evil must be conquered for us to be at one with God. Jesus, the Lion, does this by being the Lamb.

BOTH SERVANT AND LAMB

Jesus only spoke of the meaning of his death two times in the Gospels: in Mark 10:45, an echo of the Servant Songs, and in his treatise at the Last Supper, which pointed to the Passover lamb. But even these two seemingly divergent images are connected. The word for "lamb" in Aramaic can also be translated as "servant." "Lamb of God" in Greek can refer to an earlier Aramaic word, *talya*, which can be translated as "lamb," "servant," or "boy." So it's possible that John the Baptist was really proclaiming "Here is the servant of the Lord" when he saw Jesus.

The suffering servant metaphor was so deeply entwined with the life and death of Jesus that we must take seriously its ramifications for our lives today. On one hand, only Jesus can do the vicarious suffering needed to rescue Israel—and us. He alone, in his life and death, replicated the lamb of Isaiah 53. He alone is the sin-bearer. On the other hand, Jesus called his disciples, and us, to take up our crosses and follow him (Luke 9:23). We can't carry our crosses as sin-bearers, but we can give ourselves to a life that might mean suffering—a life of nonviolent love that somehow opens up the way for new life, both individually and corporately. This suffering is a natural result of our obedience, for in our obedience we too will challenge oppression and receive its pushback. This is the only way that carrying our cross has any meaning for us. If we take Jesus seriously, our atonement must incorporate a way of discipleship that includes carrying our cross.

Cleopas and his friend, walking toward Emmaus, couldn't see it. They couldn't remember Jesus' words to them that he would suffer, die, and rise again. Was this just a memory problem on their part? Or was the way of suffering so foolish to Cleopas and his friend that they couldn't comprehend Jesus' execution even though he told them it would happen? As Paul would say to the church at Corinth, "For the message about the cross is foolishness to those who are perishing, but to us who are being saved it is the power of God. . . . For Jews demand signs and Greeks desire wisdom, but we proclaim Christ crucified, a stumbling block to Jews and foolishness to Gentiles, but to those who are the called, both Jews and Greeks, Christ the power of God and the wisdom of God" (1 Corinthians 1:18, 22-24).

Perhaps the way of the cross seemed so foolish that Cleopas and his friend simply couldn't grasp its real meaning. Perhaps we, too, are sometimes unwilling to see in Christ's death not only payment for our sins but also a call to our own suffering. Are we willing to see the Messiah as he really is?

3

What Does Paul Say about Atonement?

Like us, the apostle Paul sought to untangle the mystery of the cross. And Paul had a lot to untangle. Born a Pharisee and trained under the best rabbis, Paul, at that time named Saul, saw himself as one righteous under the Jewish law. Saul also believed, as every Torah-observant Jew did, that the Messiah would come. This coming Messiah would reign in glory. The Messiah could not allow himself to be killed—and he most certainly could not be crucified on a tree. That flew in the face of Deuteronomy 21:22-23, a Scripture that declared that anyone hung on a tree was cursed.

So for Saul, the concepts of suffering and Messiah simply didn't go together. Jesus couldn't be the Messiah. Saul thus believed himself to be righteous in his active persecution of Jesus-followers.

But on the road to Damascus, the risen Jesus set him straight. Saul became Paul and went from Jesus-hater to Jesus-lover, from persecuting Christians to being persecuted himself for following Christ.

Add to this drama the fact that Paul lived in two distinct worlds. He was a devout and educated Jew who grew up in a Greek city. He had to understand and interpret a Hellenistic, or Greek, world as well as a Jewish one. These two worlds also had to survive under Roman occupation, with its own worldview. The post–Damascus road Paul was passionately convinced that Jesus was the Messiah and that his life, death, and resurrection held the key to setting the whole cosmos free from the power of sin.

How do you explain Jesus to such diverse groups? How do you explain that you follow as Lord a criminal who was executed in the most humiliating way possible—*and* that this horrible execution was all part of the plan? The cross was a major stumbling block for at least two groups, the Jews and the Greeks. It was an absolute scandal to the Jews and sheer foolishness to the Greeks.

What's an apostle to do?

METAPHORS THAT REVEAL TRUTH

One way forward in this dilemma is to use metaphors. If you're a preacher trying to reach people with a message scandalous to some and foolish to others, you take illustrations from the world of commerce, worship, the courtroom—and you use different metaphors for different groups.

Metaphors reveal truth differently than propositional statements do. Unlike a direct statement, metaphors aren't literal. Jesus isn't an actual gate (John 10) or a literal lamb (Revelation 5). But just because these images aren't literal doesn't mean they don't speak truth. They are invaluable precisely because they can communicate complex truth in ways that a direct propositional statement can't. Paul understood their power to convey the complex truth about why Jesus died as he did.

Paul used many metaphors to explain atonement. Sometimes he even used a variety of metaphors in one passage, showing the need for more than one to reveal the truth. We will look at three metaphors in depth in this chapter. Examining them, we will both uncover their brilliance and remember their limits, especially when their meanings are taken too literally or when we take only one or two and leave the others behind. Some of the metaphors found in Paul's epistles and other New Testament writings were not used by Jesus himself, but they don't challenge what Jesus said about his impending death. As we saw in chapter 2, Jesus most clearly connected himself with the Servant Songs in Isaiah and with the Passover lamb from the exodus from Egypt; the New Testament writers use the same metaphors and build upon them.

JUSTIFICATION

One of the most common metaphors is **justification**, which means being made righteous before God. This metaphor is taken from the world of law, invoking concepts of guilty and not guilty. It's a favored metaphor for many contemporary Christians, who sometimes say the word means "just as if I'd never sinned." Because it can easily become the only way of interpreting the atonement, justification must be understood in its biblical context. Our current context of a courtroom scene—in which the guilty receive their just payment and the innocent go free—isn't quite the way first-century Jews understood this term.

Many today use this metaphor and see God as the judge. Humans have sinned, and in that sin, we've broken God's law.

God, through Jesus, credited to us a legal status of being justified. We are criminals because of our sin, condemned to die. So Jesus steps in to take our place, pays the penalty, and then God forgives us. Justification, then, is something God does for you apart from anything that you could do. We accept this truth, and this is called faith. This makes justification equal to a legal pronouncement of God's acceptance, like a "not guilty" verdict in a courtroom.

When Paul thought about being justified, though, he did not see justification as a legal statement. He saw the act of being justified as being made righteous, and he saw righteousness as a state of being made right *in the context of covenant*. Where has the relationship gone wrong, and how can things be made right again? For Paul, righteousness is deeper than proclaiming someone not guilty. Relationships and behavior get changed. God's righteousness is more relational than legal. And in the context of covenant, God's righteousness opens the door for our response of gratitude. God always acts first (see Exodus 20:1; Deuteronomy 26:5-9) and then we naturally respond in gratitude and love (see Exodus 20:3-17; Deuteronomy 26:10; and Micah 6:8). God's "righteousness" (*tzadeek* in Hebrew) is God's saving activity on behalf of people.

Faith is another misunderstood word in many of our contexts today. For Paul, faith didn't mean saying yes to a set of correct beliefs, which is how many Christians today see it. For Paul, faith is akin to obedience. It is pledging allegiance to something, being reliable and loyal. To "have faith in Jesus" is to give him our allegiance. Faith is about faithfulness.

Romans 3:21-26 illustrates the point. In verse 22, the Greek word for "faith" could mean "faith in Jesus" or it could mean "the faithfulness of Jesus." In verse 26, the same distinction could be made. In the first instance, verse 22, Paul is talking about the faithfulness of Jesus—faithfulness that led him to the cross. In verse 26, Paul is referring to our trust, or faith, in Jesus.

> But now, apart from law, the righteousness of God has been disclosed, and is attested by the law and the prophets, the righteousness of God through faith in Jesus Christ [or the faithfulness of Jesus] for all who believe. For there is no distinction, since all have sinned and fall short of the glory of God; they are now justified by his grace as a gift, through the redemption that is in Christ Jesus, whom God put forward as a sacrifice of atonement by his blood, effective through faith. He did this to show his righteousness, because in his divine forbearance he had passed over the sins previously committed; it was to prove at the present time that he himself is righteous and that he justifies the one who has faith in Jesus.

It's important in any atonement discussion to see how the word *faith* can be understood in different ways. Are we saved because we have faith (believe the right things) in Jesus? Or are we saved by the faithfulness *of* Jesus?[1]

Most Christians say we're justified by our own faith. It's wonderful to trust God, and it's something I strive to do every day. But taken to its logical extension, couldn't trust become just another act of what Martin Luther called "works righteousness"—things humans do to earn salvation? I could begin to believe that I saved myself by believing in Jesus—and believing in him in the right way. It is true that the ancient understanding of faith can mean our trust in Jesus. It's a both-and, as shown in Romans 3:26. We are saved by the faithfulness of Jesus, and in that salvation, we are transformed so that we too become righteous.

It's clear that the faithfulness of Jesus was important to Paul. Earlier, in Romans 3:3, Paul asks if the faithlessness of humanity might nullify God's faithfulness, to which Paul gives a hearty "No!" God is faithful, and through Jesus, that faithfulness is crystal clear. This isn't just about a legal transaction; Jesus had been faithful all along, and the cross is the natural outcome of that faithfulness.

It doesn't take a rocket scientist to figure out that Jesus' nonconformity to economic, religious, and social structures was going to get him killed. He challenged injustice. When the **powers**—the spiritual reality of groups or systems that rebel against God—threatened Jesus with their worst weapon, death by crucifixion, he didn't flinch. The faithfulness of Jesus saved us.

So how does the cross save us, according to the justification metaphor as Paul intended it? The Protestant Reformers were right in that our justification results from a divine act of Jesus, performed apart from our actions and despite our sin. God is faithful to covenant. However, this divine act is not primarily an action declaring humanity just in the sense of a legal transaction, by crediting us with a legal righteousness. A legal declaration doesn't and can't set us free in the same sense that God acted to free the slaves from Egypt. God's *tzadeek*, or "righteousness," means God delivers humans from all kinds of oppression, physical and spiritual. This *tzadeek* created the people of God in the wilderness and a new people of God at Pentecost. Having been set free, God's people are so transformed that they can be a vessel through which God sets the world free.

So the traditional view of justification by faith is not completely wrong; it just doesn't go far enough. Our human efforts can't save us, and right belief about the atonement can't either. But we can, through the faithfulness of Christ, receive a righteousness that is much more than just a changed status in God's courthouse. We can become free to live differently, in a covenant relationship with God.

EXPIATION

Expiation is the process by which sins or impurity are cleansed or covered over. For the ancient Israelites, this was usually done in a ritual that involved a sacrifice. Paul uses the metaphor of expiation in Romans 3:25, alongside the justification metaphor (Romans 3:21-26). The Greek word is *hilasterion*, which means "mercy seat." Built on top of the ark of the covenant, the **mercy seat** was that sacred space where the loving God met a repentant people. God took initiative to deliver the people from physical bondage in Egypt and now was taking initiative again to free them from spiritual bondage. God provided mercy for a sinful people.

In the Old Testament, expiation (the Hebrew word is *kippur*) meant a "covering over" or "cleansing from" sin. While expiation could be done in a nonreligious setting, most of the time it happened in a religious ritual and almost always involved the slaying of an animal. The slain animal forfeited its life as a substitute (see Exodus 30:16). Most importantly, the merciful God was the one who expiated or atoned; God was the one who made a way. As Leviticus 17:11 states, "For the life of the flesh is in the blood; and *I have given it to you* for making atonement for your lives on the altar; for, as life, it is the blood that makes atonement" (emphasis mine).

One of the most important days of the year for the Israelites was the Day of Atonement, on which the Lord made a way for a sinful people. This ritual involved using blood to atone for the sins of the priest, his family, and the entire congregation. In other ancient religions, the people took the initiative to atone for their sins; they propitiated an angry god. But here God takes the initiative. God makes the way forward.

It's clear in both testaments that God is a holy God and that God's people need to be holy. Everything that became unclean and everyone who had transgressed needed to be expiated. Yet it was more than just doing expiation to avoid punishment. God and the people had a relationship that needed tending. All the varied rules and rituals for Old Testament atonement are too complicated to make a straightforward doctrine out of them. Yet they all point to the importance of this covenantal holiness. Righteousness and being one with God was, and is, more than just a legal status or getting cleansed. The atonement rituals weren't magic pills. The story of Saul and Samuel helps us see that obedience is what God longs for (1 Samuel 15:22). It was, and is, about relationship and transformation.

The concept of expiation took a major turn with the Hebrew people's exile to Babylon and the destruction of the temple. Without a temple there could be no blood sacrifice, and therefore atonement took on a different meaning. Two theological developments emerged: the importance of fulfilling the Law (or doing good works), and the idea of the atoning value of the innocent suffering of the righteous.

Fast-forward to the New Testament for another major shift. Hebrews 10:11-18 explains how Christ is the atoning sacrifice that is so complete, or perfect, that sacrifices are no longer necessary. Serving as both priest and sacrifice, Jesus comes to us as both Lord and victim. That moment of meeting undoes us, transforms us. Once again, God takes the initiative and provides the way out.

PROPITIATION

Hilasterion can mean either mercy seat or expiation. This connection might sound strange to our ears. Many of us are more familiar with atonement rituals done to placate a holy God who has been offended. What about the wrath of God?

Doesn't this biblical phrase—the wrath of God—prove that God is angry and needs to be appeased? And what do we do with Leviticus 17:11 and Hebrews 9:22? These verses say that without the shedding of blood, there is no forgiveness of sin. Does this mean that God can't forgive us without blood—that somehow God must have a "pound of flesh" or some other kind of retribution?

Propitiation is a term used to capture the idea of placating an angry deity. But is that what Paul meant? In Romans 3:21-26, Paul saw God, through Jesus, as the one who puts forth this expiation, this place of mercy; in this sense, expiation is different from the concept of propitiation. The direct object of expiation is sin; we expiate, or cleanse, sin. The direct object of propitiation has to be personal—an entity or being. Traditionally we've made that object to be God. Did Jesus' death on the cross expiate sin? Or did it propitiate—that is, appease—God? The King James Version of Romans 3:25 uses *propitiation* instead of *expiation*. If that translation is correct, then God, through Jesus, is not providing a mercy seat but is appeasing an angry deity. Is God appeasing himself? This seems unlikely. Simply put, the biblical text doesn't really support an angry God.

There is a striking difference between the Israelite worship of Yahweh and how other ancient religions dealt with sin and separation. In the latter, humans sought to appease their gods. Humans took the initiative, and it wasn't so much to heal the relationship as it was to avoid punishment and keep the fertility system healthy. Yet the Israelites understood *God* to be the one who provides for atonement of sin. This harks back to the Red Sea event. Yahweh took initiative when the slaves were in bondage in Egypt and showered them with grace. This mighty deliverance came at God's initiative. This pattern—of God's grace and then our gratitude—is woven throughout Scripture. "While we still were sinners Christ died for us" (Romans 5:8), and 1 John 2:1-2 says it as well: "But if anyone does sin, we have an advocate with the Father, Jesus Christ the righteous; and he is the atoning sacrifice for our sins, and not for ours only but also for the sins of the whole world."

Does the fact that we need an advocate for our relationship with the Father mean that God is angry and Jesus steps in, just in time, to save us from God's wrath? "The wrath of God" is one of the most misunderstood phrases in the Bible. Paul and other early church leaders would have connected this wrath with the concept of covenant. In the Old Testament, the phrase is specifically "wrath of Yahweh," and Yahweh is our name for God that signals covenant. In the context of covenant, Yahweh is not some impersonal, far-off deity but rather the brokenhearted Parent. Yes, there was and is wrath, but it's coming from a personal, intimate Yahweh, the Yahweh who cares for justice and right relationships for all.

God's wrath, like that of any good and loving parent, is in the context of both love and restoration. Good parents ground their teenagers when they get into risky behavior. The kids hate it, but it's the loving thing to do. Likewise, Yahweh's wrath became a way—maybe a last-ditch effort—to bring a wayward people back from the brink of destruction. Israel keeps being unfaithful, and God responds. This response honors free will. In essence, God finally lets humans have what they've been asking for. We choose to be unfaithful, and God lets the natural consequences of our rebellion take effect (see Romans 1:24, 26, 28; Ephesians 2:3). Hopefully the consequences are painful enough that we come back and get restored.

A look at Romans 5:8-11 proves the point. "But God proves his love for us in that while we still were sinners Christ died for us. Much more surely then, now that we have been justified by his blood, will we be saved through him from the wrath of God. For if while we were enemies, we were reconciled to God through the death of his Son, much more surely, having been reconciled, will we be saved by his life. But more than that, we even boast in God through our Lord Jesus Christ, through whom we have now received reconciliation."

First, we see that God proves his love for us. God practices **shalom justice**: the justice that happens when people get what they need instead of the negative punishment they deserve. God in Christ gave us what we needed—the incarnation of Jesus, which culminated in his death and resurrection and the sending of the Spirit—instead of the bad judgment we deserved. Second, we can see that being justified is deliverance that keeps us from needing God's wrath. We start to get free from our rebellion, and then we avoid suffering the consequences. Third, we are also "saved by his life" (Romans 5:10). This again affirms that our justification sets us free from our sin and doesn't just change our status with God from guilty to not guilty. And it affirms that not just Christ's death but the whole work of Christ—his life, teachings, miracles—are part of our salvation, or deliverance, from sin.

The Romans passage, as well as the whole tenor of the New Testament, tells us that expiation is not a process whereby we appease an angry God. *God* provides the means of the expiation. This is shown all over the New Testament, as Jesus comes to us because of God's first, initiating love. Jesus is our mercy seat, given to us not because we deserve it but because we need it. John 3:16 states (emphasis mine), "For God so *loved* the world that he gave his only Son, so that everyone who believes in him may not perish but may have eternal life."

SACRIFICE

The atonement metaphor of sacrifice is closely related to expiation, since expiation requires sacrifice as part of its ritual. Sacrifice was a complex affair for the ancient Hebrews. While many sacrifices were meant specifically to bring forgiveness, they were also used to offer thanks, formalize a covenant, or protect against evil. When Jesus used the sacrifice metaphor, he connected himself most fully to the Passover lamb, which was the sacrificial lamb whose blood the Israelite slaves put on their doorposts to protect them from the angel of death. Paul, on the other hand, connects Jesus' sacrifice more to the atonement lamb. Paul sees Jesus as the one who gave his life up to a vicarious, sacrificial death.

Paul writes in Philippians, "Let the same mind be in you that was in Christ Jesus, who, though he was in the form of God, did not regard equality with God as something to be exploited, but emptied himself, taking the form of a slave, being born in human likeness. And being found in human form, he humbled himself and became obedient to the point of death—even death on a cross" (Philippians 2:5-8). Jesus vicariously suffers and dies for us. But for Paul, that doesn't necessarily imply that Jesus was taking punishment from God. "Let the same mind be in you": this phrase suggests that it was for love he went to the cross.

Paul also sees the sacrifice metaphor as something applied to himself and other Jesus-followers. As they follow Jesus, Christians are to become "living sacrifices" by being nonconformed to this world (Romans 12:1-2). Paul saw himself as living in the paradox of sacrificial service to Christ (Romans 15:15-16). That Paul uses the sacrifice metaphor in different ways, and that he uses it to describe our lives as disciples, tells us that Paul didn't see only one meaning for sacrifice. We continue Christ's sacrificial life not as the means of forgiveness but as the natural consequence of discipleship. As Peter says, "Come to him, a living stone, though rejected by mortals yet chosen and precious in God's sight, and like living stones, let yourselves be built into a spiritual house, to be a holy priesthood, *to offer spiritual sacrifices* acceptable to God through Jesus Christ" (1 Peter 2:4-5, emphasis mine).

Christ's sacrifice is a once-for-all sacrifice, according to Hebrews 9:23–10:18. Jesus is both priest and sacrifice. The sacrifice is his death on the cross, yes, but even more so, the sacrifice is his obedience (Hebrews 10:7). Just like the priest did during the Day of Atonement in earlier times, Jesus enters the sanctuary; yet here, as Jesus acts as the priest, we find that it is with his own shed blood that he makes the perfect sacrifice. And this sacrifice is, in theologian John Driver's words, a "radical return to the original purpose of sacrifice in the Old Testament, that is, a means of restoring personal relationship between God and humanity."[2] By the time of first-century Judaism, sacrifice had to happen constantly, because the people kept sinning. It had also come to mean, at least for some, a mere ritual among other rituals, meaningful only to the extent that it fulfilled the Law and "saved" one from the wrath of God. So Christ's once-and-for-all sacrifice was a 180-degree turnaround. "Cultic sacrifice, then, was not merely transcended," writes Driver; "it came to an end in him."[3]

The sacrificial motif connects to Jesus' own understanding of his death as a type of ransom. He speaks of the blood of the covenant (Mark 14:24; Matthew 26:28). This renewing of the old covenant and creation of a new one comes to fruition at the Last Supper. Using phrases from Isaiah 53, Jesus blends the suffering servant imagery with the metaphor of sacrifice. The "blood and the body" is Jesus' free and voluntary self-giving, like that of the servant.

OTHER IMPORTANT METAPHORS

Paul and other New Testament writers use several other key metaphors for the atonement. Previously we've talked about Jesus as the suffering servant and Lamb of God. We saw Jesus as the one who was ransomed for us. Other metaphors in Scripture create a fuller picture: the one who adopts us, archetype, liberator, and reconciler.

One who adopts us. Jesus is the one who adopts us. Ephesians 1:5-7 states, "He destined us for adoption as his children through Jesus Christ, according to the good pleasure of his will, to the praise of his glorious grace that he freely bestowed on us in the Beloved. In him we have redemption through his blood, the forgiveness of our trespasses, according to the riches of his grace." Closely connected to the concept of redemption (Galatians 4:5), this beautiful metaphor helps us see Christ's life and death as bringing us into God's family (Hebrews 2:9-11). We have been redeemed, loved by our heavenly Parent and sisters and brothers in Christ.

Archetype. Jesus is the archetype—the second Adam, the pioneer, forerunner, and firstborn. The ancients believed that one person could represent the whole of humanity. Sometimes when one person sins, the whole community suffers (see Joshua 6–7). Likewise, one person can reverse the destiny of humankind. Paul compares Jesus, the last Adam, to the first Adam. Just as the first Adam sinned and set us on a course of sin and pain, so too Jesus, in his obedience, reverses our destiny (Romans 5:12-21). In this metaphor, the suffering and death of Jesus are viewed not as something that takes the place of our suffering and death but rather as representative. And the suffering and death of Jesus call us to the same pattern. Jesus is the firstborn (Colossians 1:15-23), and this gives him authority over all things. This title of firstborn comes primarily because of his obedience all the way to death (Philippians 2:6-11)—an obedience to which we are also called.

Liberator. Jesus is also our liberator. This word functions both as metaphor and reality for those Jesus healed and freed from demons. He began his ministry with a face-off in the wilderness, and the fight did not end until there was victory at the resurrection. Everywhere there was conflict, both with personified evil and the powers. Jesus exorcised demons and challenged the unjust systems that tried to become God. He challenged the temple system and other religious practices that oppressed people (Mark 2:1-12; 3:1-6; Matthew 12:9-14). Ironically, in the moment that he looked the weakest, Jesus defeated evil at the cross. Seemingly helpless and humiliated, the crucified Christ was the conqueror who led Satan and the powers on their own walk of humiliation and shame (Colossians 2:13-15).

Reconciler. The cross makes a way for us to be reconciled, and reconciliation is both a metaphor and a historical occurrence. Jesus reconciled feuding groups, his own band of diverse disciples being the primary example. He talked with a Samaritan woman; he healed the slave of a Roman centurion. He crossed taboo boundaries on almost every page of the Gospels. The cross, says Paul, took down the dividing wall of hostility (see Ephesians 2:14). More than a symbol, this was an actual "wall of hostility": a designated spot at the temple that signaled to Gentiles not to come any further into the temple building. If we don't understand this context, we see the cross as only eliminating the imagined hostility between us and God.

NO ONE METAPHOR IS ENOUGH

The cross of Christ has multiple meanings, as clearly shown by Paul and the other New Testament writers. And the fact that Paul uses several metaphors in one passage also tells us that these images are indeed metaphors. In Ephesians 2:11-22 alone, at least six metaphors appear.

The atonement is complicated, and it can't be explained by any one metaphor. Christ is our liberator and redeemer, the archetype and suffering servant. The cross justifies us and serves as our mercy seat. Jesus carried his cross on our behalf, and called us to carry our crosses.

The early church and theologians had to look at this complexity and try to make sense of it. How they did this—and how they relied on biblical metaphors for atonement—is our next subject.

4

What Does the Church Say about Atonement?

Lesslie Newbigin, a British missiologist who served for many years in India, wrote this parable for the Indian church:

> If I'm drowning in a well and another man jumps into the well and rescues me, while he himself is drowned in the effort, then there can be no doubt about that man's love. He has given his life for me. But if I'm attacked by a tiger, I need a different kind of help. My friend may jump into the well and drown himself, but that will not rescue me from the tiger. In that case, even though my friend gave up his life, I cannot say that he loved me or saved me. Christ gave up his life on the cross, but how does that save me? How does it rescue me from my sin? Unless we can show that there is some connection between Christ's death and my sin, I cannot believe that Christ's death is proof of love for me, or that it has saved me from sin. Clearly it is not enough simply to say that the cross is a revelation of God's love, unless we can answer these questions.[1]

Newbigin was onto something. Unless there is a clear connection between the death of Jesus and our problem with sin, the cross is as meaningless as a person jumping into a well to save someone being attacked by a tiger. Another way to think about this connection is to think about how sin breaks the four major relationships: the relationship between us and God, us and others, us and our inner selves, and us and the physical world. If sin damages these relationships, then surely salvation—the work of Jesus, which includes his death—must heal those four relationships. Or again, it's like the two families with loved ones who were alcoholic. The first family just keeps forgiving their family member week after week after week, but the second family finds a way to help their loved one get sober. The second family tames the tiger. We don't just need to be saved. We need to be healed.

MODELS OF ATONEMENT OFFERED BY THE CHURCH

The church has struggled for centuries to answer the question, How does the death of Jesus save us? This struggle has resulted in several atonement models, or theories. We will look at these various perspectives in this chapter.[2]

Models are different from metaphors, in that the models take the metaphors and use them to answer the question, How does the death of Jesus save us? Most models favor a single biblical metaphor. Proponents of a few of the models say their metaphor is the only way to understand atonement. We will not only look at each model but begin to evaluate them. Here are some of the questions we'll ask about each model:

- Does this model simply value the death of Jesus, or does it understand all of Jesus' life, teachings, death, and resurrection as connected to salvation?

- Does this model heal all four of the relationships that sin breaks or only the relationship between us and God? (In other words, does the person being attacked by a tiger get help?)
- Are the historical reasons that Jesus was executed part of this model?
- How does this model portray the character of God? Is God free to use shalom justice, or is God beholden to retributive justice?
- Does the model value the variety and complexity of all the atonement metaphors found in Scripture?
- How does this atonement model influence our understanding of discipleship and ethics?

THE CLASSIC CHRISTUS VICTOR MODEL

The early church pondered the different metaphors offered by Jesus and Paul and sensed a need to bring clarity in their context. They created systems of atonement theories, which we also call models. *Christus Victor*, "Christ the Victor" in Latin, is probably the earliest atonement model. Here Jesus saves and heals us by defeating the devil. The imagery is one of cosmic conflict, in which Jesus battles with Satan. This view, also known as the "classic view," made a direct connection with the early church because their conflict with the Roman government felt like a fight with the devil. The Christus Victor view fell out of favor after the Roman emperor Constantine became a Christian and legalized Christianity. Freed from persecution, believers had a greatly reduced need to "battle" evil powers. It now became possible to be lulled into the notion that one was a Christian simply because one was a citizen of the Roman Empire.

Recapitulation. There are two variations to this atonement model. The first variation, recapitulation, came from the church father Irenaeus (AD 130–202). He took note of the archetype metaphors that portrayed Jesus as the second Adam, and from those metaphors he developed a theory in which Jesus defeated Satan by becoming the second Adam and reversing the destiny of humankind. Adam, in his free will, sinned. As the representative human, he set the course of history for the rest of us. We would be doomed to this miserable state except that Jesus came as the second Adam and reversed, or recapitulated, our destiny, through his birth, life, teachings, death, and resurrection.

Ransom. The second version of Christus Victor was developed by Gregory of Nyssa. The scenario played out like this: Humanity was enslaved by the devil, and God put forth Jesus as the redemption payment—the ransom. The devil got Jesus and then had to set free all humankind. Gregory's social context lent itself well to this metaphor, because many people of that time were captured by gangs and held hostage.

But this view begs the question, To whom is the ransom paid? The most common answer was the devil. Origen of Alexandria (AD 184–253), another early church leader, said that the devil accepted the offer but that Jesus was so pure that it tortured Satan to have him; therefore, he let Jesus go. It was the devil's own miscalculating that led to Jesus escaping his captivity to Satan. But Gregory refuted this claim and said that God did the deceiving. God tricked Satan, hiding the divinity of Christ under the veil of his humanity. Many questioned the idea of God being deceptive, to which Gregory argued that the ends justified the means.

The Christus Victor model, with its two versions, has much in favor of it. It uses biblical metaphors, and while it seems somewhat influenced by the cultural settings that Irenaeus and Gregory found themselves in—times of persecution and many

4. What Does the Church Say about Atonement?

people being held as hostages—that influence doesn't go so far as to violate biblical truth. And both Irenaeus and Gregory affirmed the use of other biblical metaphors; they didn't claim that their metaphors were the only answers to the question of the atonement.

In the Christus Victor model, Satan and systemic evil, sometimes known as the powers, are defeated (see Ephesians 6:12). Like the biblical narrative, this model sees evil as both personal—the devil and his demons—and corporate. With Paul, this model acknowledges that evil can be incorporated into systems called powers. These systems start out as good things, but far too often they ask for allegiance that belongs only to God. The temple system is a good example. While the temple was originally designed to honor God, people started honoring the temple itself and using it to control others, culminating in the temple becoming more important than God. This led to many abuses; those who were poor or disabled—people who needed the temple the most to be forgiven and healed—couldn't even go to the temple. Those who could go paid jacked-up prices for the sacrificial animals. So Jesus challenged the "powers" of the temple, forgiving people outside the system and turning over the merchants' tables.[3]

The model connects historically with Jesus, as the Gospels show Jesus exorcizing demons, claiming victory over Satan in the wilderness and at the return of the seventy, and ultimately as the resurrection conquered death. This is good news for us, in that Jesus defeats both personal and corporate evil; the tiger is taken care of. By Jesus' defeat of evil, humanity is forgiven but also set free from sin bondage. Under this model, all four of the broken relationships can find healing, as evil in all its manifestations is taken down. We humans are changed, as opposed to God needing to be changed, as we will see happen in other models. God is not portrayed as angry or vindictive.

The resurrection plays a major role in this model. God's raising Jesus from the dead is proof that the devil and sin have been defeated. The resurrection is God's validation of Jesus, God's sign that Jesus truly defeated evil. The cross was an essential part of that defeat, but it was not the last word.

There are some weaknesses to this model, however. The idea that God needed to be deceptive to get Jesus from the clutches of the devil, or even that God needed to trick the devil in the first place, says something negative about God and seems to give the devil too much power. Why should God grant Satan that much respect?

THE SATISFACTION MODEL

Saint Anselm, living in the eleventh century, developed another way of explaining how the cross saves humanity.[4] Anselm lived in the context of feudalism: a world of kings, knights, feudal lords, and serfs. His was a world in which everyone's life was regulated by strict rules of reciprocity and honor. The underlings stood in debt to the landowners and owed them payment and the honor due a lord. The feudal lords, in turn, were required to provide safety and a meager subsistence to their serfs. Life was like a big ledger, and everything needed to be balanced. God was like the greatest of all feudal lords, Anselm maintained, and humanity, because of sin, owed such a great debt to the King that no one could pay it. And yet it had to be paid. For even God's authority was under this rule of reciprocity. God couldn't forgive his "serfs" even if God wanted to; the debt had to be paid so that God's honor would be satisfied. With this enormous, unpayable debt, all were doomed. But Jesus came, and because he was sinless, he could pay the debt and thus satisfy God's honor. Once Jesus died on the cross, God was able to forgive humans, the ledger books were balanced, and humanity was set free.

This satisfaction model is a popular atonement view among Christians, but it has many biblical problems. While all atonement theories and their authors draw from their cultures to a certain extent, Anselm allowed the feudal system to influence his atonement view more than he allowed the Bible to influence it. Some claim this theory has no biblical backing at all, while others connect it to the expiation metaphor. Romans 6:23 does say that "the wages of sin is death," but the apostle Paul was unlikely to take his understanding of expiation as far as Anselm did. And if the cross was clearly and only about expiation and a payment of debt, as this view suggests, then wouldn't it have been clear to the disciples why Jesus had to die? Wouldn't Cleopas and his friend have gotten it? If the meaning of the atonement is as plain to see as some suggest, the disciples would not have been so perplexed.

The problems? When we look at the story of Jesus, and especially the cross narratives in the Gospels, we see no hint of God needing to be satisfied. Nowhere in the Bible is God concerned about God's honor being damaged. And to say that some law has so much power that it's greater than God makes us pause. Was God truly unable to forgive us until after the death of Jesus? Jesus forgave many people before he died. God's ability to forgive is not beholden to any arbitrary law of retributive justice.

Perhaps the biggest problem with the satisfaction view is that it lives on the edge of history. This means our sin problem is nothing but a debt that gets taken care of in the heavenly realms and that, through the cross, God is changed. God was unable to forgive us, and now God can. So our salvation gives no hope for our terrible bondage to addictions or self-hatred or our inability to love our neighbor. God is changed, and our relationship with God is healed. But the other relationships? We are still enslaved.

Penal substitutionary atonement. The penal substitutionary view is a cousin, of sorts, to the satisfaction model. This understanding of the atonement is a foundational pillar for many American churches nurtured in the language of popular praise and worship songs. The landscape of this model changes from feudalism to the courtroom, but the basic principles are similar. Proponents of the penal substitutionary atonement view argue that a just God can't forgive humans for violations without punishment. In this view, a holy God couldn't forgive our sin without the death of Jesus even if God had wanted to. God has to be morally consistent, so someone must be punished.

Even more, this model suggests, our sin incurs wrath from God. God, as the angry judge, can't overlook our sin. But Jesus comes to our rescue. Jesus bears the wrath of God as our substitute. Jesus bears our guilt and suffers punishment, resulting in his death on the cross. In this way, God can have what God needs—moral consistency—and God can now look at us with different eyes and forgive us because of Jesus.

Paul does use metaphors like justification and expiation to explain the cross, as we have seen. We read about the transgression of the law and the wrath of God. But as we saw earlier, the wrath of God can also be seen as God allowing the natural consequences of our sin to find us. And when Paul spoke of justification, he was thinking about the covenants God made with Israel—covenants that don't follow a strict tit-for-tat, punishment-must-fit-the-crime kind of thinking. The Old Testament word for covenant love is *chesed*, which translates into English as "steadfast love." Yet even that term hardly contains the fullness of the word. *Chesed* represents all those times that God had every right to walk away from the people and didn't.

Problems with the penal substitutionary view also abound. In this model, *God's* heart needs to be changed, not ours. God needs help dealing with anger, and thankfully Jesus quenches that anger. What does that say about the relationship between God and Jesus? Does the rest of the Bible communicate that God is angry? When Jesus says that "God so loved the world that he gave his only Son" (John 3:16), it would suggest something else entirely.

The Bible shows God using shalom justice, not retributive justice. Again, in shalom justice, people receive what they need instead of what they deserve. The most beautiful picture of this comes in the parable of the prodigal son, in which the father, who represents God, overwhelms his wayward son with grace and forgiveness even before his son asks for it.

According to the penal substitutionary view, the father in this story should have met the son with death threats. That's what the son deserved. At the very least, he should have been treated as a slave. But no. The father wraps his arms around the son and throws a party for him, giving him so much grace that the older brother struggles to accept it.

Did we deserve the love Jesus showed on the cross? Of course not. But it surely is what we needed. Followers of Jesus are to practice this shalom justice as well; God asks us to love and forgive our enemies while they are still our enemies. If this is true, then surely God is also capable of doing these things. Is God calling us to a greater love than God is willing to give?

Defenders of this view often emphasize the substitution part of the equation. Jesus, as God, took God's wrath, so Jesus was not so much a way to persuade God as a gift *from* God *to*

God. And in this way, God's justice can be maintained along with God's love. This concept is helpful, as it softens the seeming disconnect between the character of God and the character of Jesus. But the problems remain. Penal substitutionary atonement, like the satisfaction model, only heals our broken relationship with God. Our sin debt gets paid, but the other broken relationships are forgotten.

In this view, salvation becomes some legal transaction in the skies and has little bearing on our lives. One can "get saved" and continue doing wicked things. Taken to its logical extension, salvation becomes just a ticket to heaven, or fire insurance from hell.

THE MORAL INFLUENCE MODEL

Peter Abelard, a French theologian who lived in the twelfth century, rejected Anselm's view and created his own atonement theory: the moral influence model. Sometimes called the subjective view, this theory emphasizes the love shown on the cross. Humans—both the original crowd at Golgotha and today—are drawn to the innocent suffering of Jesus. We are stopped in our tracks when we see what we're capable of: the torture and execution of an innocent man. God is loving us back with this beautiful act of love.

There are many good things to say about this view. Like Christus Victor, this model suggests that all aspects of our lives are affected by sin and thus by salvation—our ethics, and our relationships with God, others, ourselves, and creation. Humans are the ones who get changed in this view, not God, as we move away from our wickedness and become new persons. With Jesus as our example, we become free. The author of 1 Peter, working with the difficult topic of suffering, states, "For to this you have been called, because Christ also suffered for you, leaving you an *example, so that you should follow in his steps*" (1 Peter 2:21, emphasis mine). It is this glorious example, culminating in Jesus' death, that saves us.

But we must ask the question, Is an example, even the great example of Christ, enough to save us? Is that all it takes? And if it is, why can't the life and assassination of another noble person—Martin Luther King Jr., for example—do the same thing? Couldn't secular thinkers hold this same view?

These three models—Christus Victor, satisfaction, and moral influence—represent the three major understandings of the atonement in the church.

THE NONVIOLENT ATONEMENT MODEL

New theories or variations on the three classic atonement models can help guide us through the mystery of how the cross saves us. One such theory comes from Anabaptist theologian J. Denny Weaver, who has taken the classic Christus Victor and worked to show how Jesus' victory over evil is not only a cosmic battle but also a historical one—a battle with evil that begins in real time. Using the term *narrative Christus Victor*, Weaver reminds us that the narrative of Jesus is the central interpretative key to understanding atonement. As Jesus exorcized demons and challenged systemic evil, we too find ourselves fighting—and winning—against the powers. It's not that there isn't a cosmic battle; it's just that Irenaeus and others, according to Weaver, spiritualized the battle too much. The primary battle against evil exists in real history, and Jesus defeating the powers with nonviolent love provides the key for us to continue this real-life victory.

Weaver helps us see how misguided views of the atonement can seem to validate violence. If Jesus *had* to die—a claim most other atonement views take—then it seems logical that violence has some value. God needed to do violence or at least allow it to bring atonement. Seeing atonement in this way makes it easier for us to justify our own use of violence.

A major contribution of Weaver's work is to demonstrate how Jesus defeats Satan without violence, which is why this theory is sometimes called the nonviolent view. The only way to fight evil, says Jesus, is to fight it with love. This seems counterintuitive to the world's way of thinking; it feels like surrender. But Jesus' going to the cross nonviolently, and loving even the soldiers crucifying him, was congruent with the whole of his life. And in all of that, evil gets defeated.

Colossians 2:13-15 explains this phenomenon well: "And when you were dead in trespasses and the uncircumcision of your flesh, God made you alive together with him, when he forgave us all our trespasses, erasing the record that stood against us with its legal demands. He set this aside, nailing it to the cross. He disarmed the rulers and authorities and made a public example of them, triumphing over them in it."

Here the writer of Colossians is talking about a Roman triumph. After a victory the Romans would parade the defeated general through the most crowded streets of the city, marching him and other captives to their executions. The general would stand in the middle of four soldiers, and at certain points along the way, they would flog him. Interestingly, a similar parade would be put on for the coronation of the new emperor, with a bull in the middle of the soldiers that would later be slaughtered as part of the coronation ceremony. This Roman triumph happened to Jesus on the way to Calvary. But, says Paul in Colossians, even though in the physical world Jesus was in the middle, in the spiritual world it's actually evil and all its forces in the middle. Ironically, as the powers sought to kill Jesus, they were being marched to their own defeat.

4. What Does the Church Say about Atonement?

The cross "disarmed the rulers and authorities" (the powers), triumphing over them.

Revelation supports this strategy for defeating evil. In Revelation 5, John wept when no one was found worthy to open the scroll and make history come out right. But one of the elders said, "See, the Lion of the tribe of Judah, the Root of David, has conquered, so that he can open the scroll" (Revelation 5:5). But when John looked, he didn't see a Lion but a Lamb—even more, it was a Lamb that had been slaughtered and yet was standing! The Lion symbolized victory over evil. But because *Lion Jesus* is also the *Lamb*, this means that he could only conquer evil by being the Lamb. And the Lamb? It represents sacrificial, nonviolent love.

And what is true for Jesus is true for us too. Revelation 12:11 says, "But they have conquered him [Satan] by the blood of the Lamb and by the word of their testimony, for they did not cling to life even in the face of death." The vision of Revelation makes it clear that Christians defeat the devil by being willing to be martyrs.

In the narrative Christus Victor view of atonement, the battle with evil is both here on earth and in the heavenly realms. In both places and in all ways, the way to defeat the devil is through nonviolent love, a love that plays itself out in every aspect of Jesus' life and in the way he approached his death. And because Jesus, as the very Word of God, is the norm for both ethics and theology, any atonement theory that doesn't put Jesus and his nonviolent love in the center is a view that falls short.[5]

All three of the primary atonement models play themselves out in congregations today. The moral influence view holds sway among many liberal mainline Protestants, even as the penal substitutionary atonement model captivates many conservative evangelical Christians. Anabaptists lean toward a nonviolent Christus Victor view, with an emphasis on embracing all the metaphors of the atonement. Newer voices add much to the conversation. Theologian James Cone helps us see Jesus' suffering on the cross reenacted in our own oppressive systems. The cross asks for more than just contemplation or adoration; it wakes us up to our own acts of brutality, such as the lynchings of African Americans in the United States. Like God, we are to be present with those suffering—and not only that but, in Cone's words, we are to "take the crucified down from the tree."[6] Other atonement theories—Black, feminist and womanist—also ask new questions and challenge our presumed ideas.[7]

DO WE NEED A SCAPEGOAT?

So is God angry with us? Is that why Jesus had to die? Both the satisfaction model and the penal substitutionary atonement model would suggest that God is angry. We saw some of the problems with that view. But what if *we* are the angry ones? What if Jesus had to die to show us how our entire system of rivalry, violence, and anger is wrong?

Anthropologist René Girard has been helpful in giving us another way of looking at the death of Jesus. In his research on societies, he coined the term *triangular rivalry*. We want something, and someone else wants the same thing. When we figure out that the other person wants what *we* want, we tend to want that thing even more. It's a triangle: the two rivals and the object of their desire. This causes tension and eventually violence—think Cain and Abel—so that this rivalry becomes heated.

Enter the concept of sacrifice and the scapegoat. When mob violence threatens, you find a victim to sacrifice; this satisfies the crowd's desire for revenge. Things calm down. Ironically, many times the victim is then made into a holy person. This process, says Girard, is the foundation of all religions. The death of the victim appeases the angry gods and unites the rivals. Violence, at least at some level, is justified as a needed way to release tension and keep mass violence at bay.

Girard found key differences between the Hebrew Bible and the scriptures of other religions. In Israel's rituals, the sacrificial being was an animal, not a human. And in Israel's stories, when the victim was human, this victim was innocent; in other religions, the victim had some kind of fault that justified the violence. Joseph was a type of scapegoat, and even though he was innocent, he was sold into slavery by his jealous brothers (Genesis 37). Even more, the Old Testament contains stories in which the victim forgave his oppressors, such as when Joseph forgave his brothers (Genesis 45).

Enter Jesus. He destroys the lie that says the victim deserves his fate, because it's clear that Jesus is innocent. He unmasks the whole scapegoating system as wrong and unnecessary. His death is a renunciation of violence. In truth, it is Israel—all of us—who are the guilty ones, not the victim (Jesus). Once we see that our violent, scapegoating system is so evil it would even murder God, we are stopped in our tracks. We join the Roman centurion and say, "Truly this man was God's Son!" (Matthew 27:54).

The book of Hebrews declares that Jesus' sacrifice is the sacrifice that ends all sacrifices (see Hebrews 9:23–10:18). So was the death of Jesus a sacrifice? Yes, but not a sacrifice that appeases an angry God. It was a sacrifice of love—a sacrifice that woke us up to the truth. When the Calvary crowd saw that they had crucified an innocent man, the cross functioned like a mirror that revealed evil for what it truly was. When we finally see the cross for the scandal it really is—the murder of

God—we're done, says Girard. We get it. The whole scapegoating system is seen in its true light. Jesus gave the sacrifice of obedience—an obedience that went all the way to the cross and put an end to the broken system of ritual sacrifice (see Psalm 40:6; Hosea 6:6; Matthew 9:13).

DO WE "GET" THE ATONEMENT—OR DOES IT TRANSFORM US?

All these atonement models attempt to answer the question, How does the death of Jesus save us? The models can all serve as valuable tools for our faith. But we simply cannot formulate the scandal of the cross into one neat, rational summary that explains in three steps how the execution of Jesus more than two thousand years ago saves us. On some level, no one can fully explain the mystery of the atonement.

Yet something happened through the death of Jesus; we know it, we feel it. We are becoming free. We are being rescued from the tiger. We are getting sober. We are not only enjoying forgiveness from our sins—we're living radically free, changed lives, more and more every day.

What if we understood atonement not so much as a model but as a mysterious action that God does to us and for us? Theologian James Alison explains atonement in this way: "Having atonement as a theory means that it is an idea that can be grasped—and once it is grasped, one has got it—whereas a liturgy is something that *happens at you*."[8] With atonement as a theory, we think we're in control. If we see atonement as liturgy—a form of worship—we realize we are *undergoing* atonement, not just understanding it. Something is happening to us—something good, even if it makes us feel a bit less stable or certain. Something is grabbing us, changing us. We are being transformed.

It's tempting to attach ourselves to a simplistic view of what happened on the cross when Jesus died. But what would it mean to embrace the mysterious work of the cross happening inside us and in the world? Would we become not only saved but healed? Would we find both forgiveness and restoration? Would we be reconciled not only to God but also to our enemies? Would we find the kingdom of God in our midst, find salvation starting now and not just in heaven?

5

How Does Atonement Transform Us?

So let's say that we are back on my porch, having had a long conversation about Jesus, and now we're standing in silence. The gospel booklet is still flapping in the wind. The metaphors, the models, the hundreds of Bible verses float through our heads. What do we make of all this?

It's important to put Jesus at the center of our atonement understanding. Who Jesus was is who God is (see John 1:18; 8:58). How Jesus brought atonement, or "at-one-ment," between us and God, as well as between us and others, ourselves, and creation, is key to understanding his death on the cross.

SALVATION AND HEALING

Perhaps another story from Jesus' life can help us. Luke 8:40-48 tells the story of a woman who had been having her period continuously for twelve years. This kind of bleeding wouldn't kill a woman, but it would make her anemic and keep her from being a mother, an important role and honor in the time of Jesus. Menstruation also meant you were ritually unclean. You couldn't go to the synagogue to worship; you couldn't be touched by anyone, because you would make them impure. This poor woman hadn't been touched, even by her husband, for twelve years. It's quite possible he had already left her.

She was desperate: physically sick and socially marginalized. She had spent all her money on physicians, and no one could help her. She was lonely and tired. So she did the unthinkable. She entered the busy streets because she heard Jesus, a miracle worker, was in town. She would risk touching people, making them unclean and mad at her. She would risk making even Jesus unclean by touching him. She believed him to be the Messiah, and the Messiah had healing powers in his prayer shawl. She would have to rub shoulders with others to get to him, and she would have to touch the edge of his shawl to be healed.

The crowd was heavier than she expected. But there he was, Rabbi Jesus. Before she lost her courage, she knelt and reached for his prayer shawl, catching the sacred fringe. And it happened. Her bleeding stopped. A tingle went down her spine. She was healed.

But she was also caught. "Who touched me?" Jesus said. She hardly dared to look up, but the crowd had parted, and suddenly she was the center of attention. Trembling, she fell down before Jesus and spilled her story. Every last detail. Most of the crowd knew she was unclean anyway.

"Daughter, your faith has made you well [*sozo*, in Greek]. Go in shalom." The Greek word **sozo** can mean "made well" or "be saved."

No anger from the rabbi? No shame? And she was now saved? Made well and given shalom? **Shalom**, a Hebrew term often translated "peace," actually means much more than what peace might suggest. Old Testament scholar Perry Yoder says that shalom has three variations of meaning: physical shalom, social shalom, and moral-ethical shalom. For there to be true physical shalom, everyone must have enough to eat, a decent place to sleep, and freedom from fear and poverty. The earth should be treated with care. This part of shalom is connected to the problem of sin breaking our relationship with the physical world. Social shalom refers to healthy and harmonious relationships between individuals, families, societies, and nations. More than just the absence of war, this type of shalom is deeply concerned with justice and the healing of relationships for all persons. Here shalom seeks to heal the broken relationship between us and other humans. Finally, moral-ethical shalom means that one has no deceit and is blameless. There can be no shalom if there are falsehoods and hypocrisy. This area of shalom seeks to heal the relationship between us and our inner selves.

Back to the story: Jesus did save this woman. She was healed, physically and socially. Jesus orchestrated the event so that her community would hear that she had been healed and was no longer an outcast. The woman probably needed that social healing as much as she needed the physical healing. Her neighbors had to see her differently. She had to see *herself* differently. The shame was gone. And while the story doesn't say it in so many words, my sense is that she was also reconciled to God that day.

So Jesus saved her, healing not only her relationship with God but also her relationship with others, her inner self, and the physical world. And Jesus did this all *before* he died on the cross. Does that mean that we can be made one with God without the cross? Does this story mean that Jesus didn't have to die to save us?

Some Christians see this as an important question to ask. They can see the problems that a wrong emphasis on the cross can bring. Even though Jesus was nonviolent, violence must be okay for us to use, since God needed violence to bring atonement. Or we wrongly believe that God is mean and vindictive, that God is the one who killed Jesus. Or the cross becomes simply some legal transaction in the heavenly realms, and all we have to do is say yes to get our sins forgiven. Salvation becomes our fire insurance from hell and our ticket into heaven. The deal is done and we can go about our business as usual, being just as mean and hateful as we were before. So let's ask the question again, once and for all: Why bother with the cross?

WE STILL NEED THE CROSS

Some atonement theories go there, or at least hint at the idea that the cross wasn't specifically needed. With his narrative Christus Victor model, J. Denny Weaver discusses the necessity of Jesus' death in the sense that it was the natural outcome of who Jesus was. If Jesus was going to continue threatening both Rome and the religious authorities, and if he was going to continue to be nonviolent, one can see that he was going to get killed. In that sense, and only in that sense, Jesus "needed" to die.

But what if the cross really did need to happen? As we grapple with the stories in the Gospels and the words of the apostle Paul, the centrality of the cross becomes clear. Both claim the paradox: humans killed Jesus, and God willed it. The Gospels name the Pharisees, Herodians, and Sadducees as groups who worked to see that Jesus was killed, and they also

5. How Does Atonement Transform Us?

report Jesus seeing himself as a ransom, knowing that he had to undergo great suffering. Luke has Jesus intentionally setting his face toward Jerusalem (9:51), and he also attributes Jesus' betrayal to Satan entering Judas. Luke 24 tells of Cleopas and his friend learning from the mysterious stranger (who turns out to be the resurrected Christ) that Jesus had to die to fulfill Scriptures (v. 27). Peter, in Acts 2, speaks of this paradox: "This man, handed over to you *according to the definite plan and foreknowledge of God, you* crucified and killed" (Acts 2:23, emphasis mine).

It is possible to accept that God, in some sense, *willed* Jesus' death without saying God *required* his death to satisfy God's honor. God willed it for a different reason: so that sin could truly be defeated. Jesus could only break the power of evil by entering into the worst that sin could do—kill God—and refusing to retaliate. This act broke the power of evil, unmasking it for what it really was.[1]

The cross is also important because it is our primary way of understanding God. So many people, from the Old Testament times until today, have misunderstood God, and it's a testament to God's love that God stays with us despite our confusion and sin. God's people have made horrible mistakes—forming a monarchy, allowing polygamy, praising Yahweh for being warlike, attacking innocent people in "holy" crusades—and God didn't reject them. The Spirit worked tirelessly to reveal the truth while still honoring human free will. Even at the cross, where people did the worst they could do—murder God—God stayed in the game. The cross shows that God will go all the way to be with us, despite our misunderstandings, and in this way, the cross more than anything else reveals the true nature of God. Love—God—went all the way to the cross. This is how the cross is the glory of God (John 12:23), and this is how humanity will be drawn to Jesus (John 12:32). We finally see God. And we know this love is all-powerful through the resurrection. The empty tomb is the sign of complete victory, where God roars out that the battle over evil has been won (1 Corinthians 15:54b-57).

Taking the cross out of the picture—of salvation, healing, forgiveness, and union with God—can have negative ramifications. If we're not careful, then it becomes all about us. We see the great example of Jesus, we are moved by his love, we accept the high standard of nonviolence . . . and then we try to do all this good work on our own strength. We grit our teeth and we become disciples. We clench our fists and dig in our heels, working to become good people. Without denigrating the importance of discipleship, we can see that it's simply wrong and foolish to try to transform ourselves.

There are two ditches to avoid. We can call one the "cheap grace" ditch, in which the cross functions merely to change our guilty status before God the judge, and once that status is changed, we're good to go. This is a potential pitfall of the penal substitutionary model. We don't have to be transformed; we've been forgiven, and that's all that matters.

But we must also avoid another ditch—we could call it the "earn my way to heaven" ditch—in which we transform ourselves. Christians living by the moral influence model, or even the Christus Victor model wrongly understood, are susceptible to falling into this ditch. We don't need the transforming work of the cross; we have the example of Jesus, we think, and that's enough. Here we get bogged down in our own self-righteousness, or struggle with depression when our do-gooder discipleship feels overwhelming. We focus so much on the good we must do that we stop relying on the mysterious, gracious way of Jesus, who does the transformation.

Jesus is the only one who can.

The Bible has given us many metaphors for the atonement for good reasons. The multiplicity of metaphors helps us embrace mystery and keeps us humble. It's impossible to make a grid that fits all the atonement symbols in Scripture into one coherent piece. Perhaps God never intended the Bible to give us one logical schema for the atonement. Perhaps rather than convincing us of the rightness of one understanding of the cross, God instead longs for us to be joined to Christ in life and in death. God longs for us to step into the mystery.

SHARING THE GOSPEL

Having so many biblical metaphors for the atonement can aid in our cross-cultural sharing of the gospel. Different metaphors have resonance depending on the culture in which we are reading Scripture. Missionary David Shenk writes about his experience with East African Christians and their endeavors to help people find Jesus: "I assigned my students to meet their grandparents who knew pre-Christian community in Kenya and ask, 'How did your tribe restore peace when relations had been broken?' I have seventy term papers from every tribe in Kenya. All the papers centered on substitutionary sacrifice. No exceptions. Each paper described the quest for the perfect, innocent substitute."

And yet, Shenk goes on to explain, these Christians didn't take the penal substitutionary atonement model too far when they applied it to the life and death of Christ. They understood Jesus' substitutionary sacrifice to be a life-changing event, not just a legal transaction. The Lamb of God turned them into the people of the Lamb. Says Shenk, "The revivalists in East Africa were often nicknamed the People of the Lamb. In times of war, many revivalists were slain for their insistence that a follower of the Lamb breaks the cycle of violence by absorbing the violence and forgiving."[2]

Other cultures will resonate with other biblical metaphors. Missionary C. Norman Kraus recalls how the penal substitutionary atonement model didn't work as well in a Japanese context because of the culture's understanding of justice, shame, and guilt. Kraus discovered that guilt, a foundational concept in the penal substitutionary model, made little sense in Japan's shame-based culture. In this context, people longed for a Jesus who would love them enough to vicariously suffer in shame. The cross was a way to be free from shame, which is truly good news in this context.[3]

So we hold on to the many and varied biblical metaphors for atonement. Each of them is a gift, offering another lens through which to view the work of Christ in his life, death, and resurrection. As they function together, we see a God of love and mercy. We see our own call to pick up our crosses and become living sacrifices. We see all of Jesus helping us experience an "at-one" relationship with God.

JESUS AT THE CENTER

Even though atonement is ultimately a mystery, we do have guideposts. Jesus must be at the center. We must incorporate the historical reasons that Jesus was killed, for we are to be like Jesus. Our atonement view must influence our choices and habits; otherwise we are merely saying, "Lord, Lord," and ignoring God's will (Matthew 7:21-23). On the other hand, our salvation must be more than good works, for Matthew also tells us that not everyone who prophesies and casts out demons has the "real thing" either.

Ultimately, atonement is about relationship: being in covenant with God. We must insist on the kind of atonement in

5. How Does Atonement Transform Us?

which all four of our relationships are being healed. God, through Jesus, wants to both save us and heal us.

And in our healing, we see our call to help Jesus heal the whole world. Jesus, through the Spirit and through the church, is still in the business of atonement. As Paul makes clear, this work of atonement goes on through the church:

> But now in Christ Jesus you who once were far off have been brought near by the blood of Christ. For he is our peace; in his flesh he has made both groups into one and has broken down the dividing wall, that is, the hostility between us. He has abolished the law with its commandments and ordinances, that he might create in himself one new humanity in place of the two, thus making peace, and might reconcile both groups to God in one body *through the cross*, thus putting to death that hostility through it. So he came and proclaimed peace to you who were far off and peace to those who were near; for through him both of us have access in one Spirit to the Father." (Ephesians 2:13-18, emphasis mine)

The work of atonement continues. Not only did the cross heal our relationship with God; Christ has broken down the hostility, or the walls that divide us. God continues to fix the sin problem through the church. The solution to our terrible bondage to personal and systemic evil is deeply connected to that one momentous day at Golgotha, although it extends beyond that day too. The work of atonement continues as people choose to be in relationship with Jesus, a relationship that manifests itself in the church.

God is healing the world through the church. Just as the cross brought together Jews and Gentiles—a miracle in first-century Palestine, given their deep animosity—so that work of reconciliation, via the cross, is ours today. Jesus lived, died, and rose again, but this doesn't mean that atonement has happened for all people. People are dying to "get sober" from sin. People are being eaten alive by "tigers." People are desperate for all their relationships to be healed, desperate to become channels of healing themselves. God intends for the church to be so attractive in its radical love, so transformative as rival groups worship together and live in community, so beautiful as it brings shalom to all and fights evil nonviolently, that people push down the church doors to get in.

We all long to find "at-oneness" with God. We long to be healed and not just saved. When this transformation happens, and as our relationship with Jesus grows, it's easy to carry our own crosses. It's a joy. As we have been reconciled to God, we naturally work at reconciliation with others, with creation, and with our inner selves. We naturally seek to help the world find this "at-oneness" too.

May the work of Christ, the atonement, be made manifest in us all.

Glossary

atonement: The work of Jesus Christ, in a broad sense, that brings us into union with God. Often refers more specifically to a theory about the meaning of Jesus' death on the cross.

chesed: A Hebrew word that shares a range of meanings. Many English translations render it as "steadfast love." *Chesed* is not just kindness in general; there is always a relationship involved. God shows *chesed* when God chooses to stay in covenant relationship with a disobedient people; therefore, this unconditional lovingkindness from God is undeserved.

covenant: In the biblical world, covenant refers to a formal relationship between God and an individual, a group, or groups. A biblical covenant is not the same as a business contract as we know it today, because a covenant contains a relational element. In this sense, covenants are more akin to our concept of marriage.

expiation, mercy seat, and propitiation: Three translations of one Greek word, *hilasterion*. *Expiation* means "covering" or "cleansing" from sin. Humans or God can expiate (or cleanse) sin. Another English translation of this Greek word is "mercy seat," which recalls the place in the holy of holies where God's saving mercy was supremely manifested. *Propitiation* refers to humans initiating something—a ritual sacrifice, for example—in order to appease an angry god. There is much theological debate as to the legitimacy of "propitiation" as a proper translation for *hilasterion*.

patron-client system: The rigid hierarchy of the Roman world of first-century Palestine, in which persons were sorted into categories. Hierarchy, social status, and honor were cherished values. It is into this world of patron-client hierarchy that Jesus called himself a servant and called his disciples to be the same.

powers: The spiritual reality of groups or systems that rebel against God and produce systemic evil. Paul uses political and cosmic language to describe this reality: politically, the powers are called "principalities and powers" or the "rulers and authorities" (see Ephesians 2:1-2; 6:12 KJV; Colossians 2:15); in cosmic terms, Paul talks about angels and spiritual elements. Some biblical scholars say that the powers killed Jesus. By refusing to react violently, Jesus defeated and disarmed the powers through his death and resurrection (Colossians 2:13-15).

salvation: Central Christian theological concept meaning rescue, or deliverance, of humans from spiritual and physical bondage by Jesus Christ. One who is saved is being transformed into the likeness of Christ. Some Christians understand salvation to refer to a future event, such as being with Jesus after one's death, and while it surely is that, the Bible implies that it is more. The apostle Paul talks about being saved as something that can happen to a person in the past ("I was saved"), in the future ("I will be saved"), and as an ongoing experience ("I am being saved"). All that salvation entails will come to the cosmos at the end of the ages, and yet this deliverance has begun now.

shalom: Hebrew term often translated "peace," which fails to fully illustrate biblical shalom; a better translation might be "the way God intended things to be." Shalom actually has three variations of meaning: physical shalom, social shalom, and moral-ethical shalom. Shalom happens when the relationships between humans and God, humans and others, humans and their inner beings, and humans and the physical world are being healed.

shalom justice: The most prevalent kind of justice in the Bible, related to the biblical understanding of grace. Shalom justice happens when people get what they need instead of the negative punishment they deserve.

***sozo*:** Greek word that can be translated into a variety of English words and phrases, including "to be saved"; "to be kept safe and sound"; "to be spiritually delivered, physically healed, or restored to health." Soteriology, the study of salvation, finds its origin in this word.

Discussion and Reflection Questions

INTRODUCTION

1. What is the explanation you've heard most often for why Jesus died on the cross? Have you ever wondered where that explanation came from?

CHAPTER 1

1. Do you know Christians who are "saved but not healed"? How can a limited view of atonement contribute to us being stuck in a "just saved" kind of life?
2. How was sin defined in your childhood? Your young adult years? Has this definition changed for you? How?
3. What is the difference between "Jesus was killed" and "Jesus died"? Why is it important to accept both meanings?

4. What does it mean to "carry our cross" (see Luke 9:23-25)? In what ways do you need encouragement from the Spirit to help you carry your cross?
5. Which one of the four relationships—with God, others, self, and creation—seems the most broken and in the most need of healing for you?

CHAPTER 2

1. How does Luke 4:18-19 define Jesus' mission? What do these verses imply about salvation? If you told your congregation that this was their mission too, what would they say?
2. Slowly and prayerfully read 1 Peter 2:22-25. Then journal about what Jesus is saying to you through these phrases:
   - "When he suffered, he did not threaten..."
   - "He bore our sins in his body on the cross..."
   - "By his wounds you have been healed..."
3. Pretend you're on the road to Emmaus. What parts of the cross, Jesus, and discipleship are you "accidentally on purpose" blind to?

CHAPTER 3

1. Paul uses many metaphors to describe atonement. Sometimes he uses multiple metaphors in one passage (see, for example, Ephesians 2:11-22; Colossians 2:13-15). What might Paul be saying about the atonement?
2. Are we saved because we have faith in Jesus or because of the faithfulness of Jesus? Or both?
3. What's the difference between expiation and propitiation? How does this difference change your understanding of atonement?

4. What is your favorite atonement metaphor from the writings of Paul? Why are you drawn to it?

CHAPTER 4

1. Lesslie Newbigin writes, "Unless there is a clear connection between the death of Jesus and our problem with sin, the cross is as meaningless as a person jumping into a well to save someone being eaten by a tiger." How do you see Jesus freeing you from your "tiger"?
2. Consider the main models of atonement in this chapter: Christus Victor, satisfaction, and moral influence. Which one are you most familiar with? Which one holds sway in your local congregation? Which one do you see in songs your congregation sings?
3. What's the difference between shalom justice and retributive justice? Use the parable of the prodigal son, Luke 15:11-32, to evaluate the satisfaction view.
4. What would change in you if you understood the atonement not as a doctrine to be argued about but as a mystery that transforms us?

CHAPTER 5

1. Which of the two "ditches" are you most likely to fall into: the "cheap grace" ditch or the "earn my way to heaven" ditch? What are some ways you can find balance?
2. How is the cross still tearing down the dividing walls of hostility? Consider different contexts: your family, your congregation, your community, the world.
3. Understanding atonement and experiencing atonement are both important. What is your growing edge?

Shared Convictions

Mennonite World Conference, a global community of Christian churches that facilitates community between Anabaptist-related churches, offers these shared convictions that characterize Anabaptist faith. For more on Anabaptism, go to ThirdWay.com.

By the grace of God, we seek to live and proclaim the good news of reconciliation in Jesus Christ. As part of the one body of Christ at all times and places, we hold the following to be central to our belief and practice:

1. God is known to us as Father, Son and Holy Spirit, the Creator who seeks to restore fallen humanity by calling a people to be faithful in fellowship, worship, service and witness.
2. Jesus is the Son of God. Through his life and teachings, his cross and resurrection, he showed us how to

be faithful disciples, redeemed the world, and offers eternal life.

3. As a church, we are a community of those whom God's Spirit calls to turn from sin, acknowledge Jesus Christ as Lord, receive baptism upon confession of faith, and follow Christ in life.

4. As a faith community, we accept the Bible as our authority for faith and life, interpreting it together under Holy Spirit guidance, in the light of Jesus Christ to discern God's will for our obedience.

5. The Spirit of Jesus empowers us to trust God in all areas of life so we become peacemakers who renounce violence, love our enemies, seek justice, and share our possessions with those in need.

6. We gather regularly to worship, to celebrate the Lord's Supper, and to hear the Word of God in a spirit of mutual accountability.

7. As a world-wide community of faith and life we transcend boundaries of nationality, race, class, gender and language. We seek to live in the world without conforming to the powers of evil, witnessing to God's grace by serving others, caring for creation, and inviting all people to know Jesus Christ as Saviour and Lord.

In these convictions we draw inspiration from Anabaptist forebears of the 16th century, who modelled radical discipleship to Jesus Christ. We seek to walk in his name by the power of the Holy Spirit, as we confidently await Christ's return and the final fulfillment of God's kingdom.

Adopted by Mennonite World Conference General Council, March 15, 2006

Notes

Chapter 1

1 In the past, Christians have used this cross-bearing metaphor to justify their own brand of oppression. Christians in power have insisted that other people—the people groups they wanted to conquer—bear their cross as Jesus said and submit to them as their superiors and authorities. The conquering Christians, on the other hand, had the convenience of understanding the death of Jesus in another way. David Batstone gives us one example. "The conquistadors worked with two images of Christ. The *Jesus* they gave to the indigenous groups of Latin America was the suffering, passive Jesus. They were encouraged to identify with Jesus by suffering. Then the conquistadors used another *Jesus*, an image of a conquering warrior, to justify their oppression against the indigenous groups. Conveniently, their triumphant Jesus allowed them to oppress others, and at the same time, encourage those oppressed people to 'be like Jesus' and take the oppression." See David Batstone, *From Conquest to Struggle: Jesus of Nazareth in Latin America* (Albany: SUNY Press, 1991), 14–18.

Chapter 2

1 See 4 Maccabees 17:21-22.

Chapter 3

1. This question of how to translate this phrase—as "faith in Christ" or "faithfulness of Christ"—has absorbed New Testament scholars for some time. To read more about this conversation, see N. T. Wright's commentary on Romans in *The New Interpreter's Bible*, vol. 10 (Nashville: Abingdon Press, 2002), 464–78.
2. John Driver, *Understanding the Atonement for the Mission of the Church* (Scottdale, PA: Herald Press, 1986), 142.
3. Ibid.

Chapter 4

1. Lesslie Newbigin, *Sin and Salvation* (Philadelphia: Westminster, 1956), 72.
2. Lutheran theologian Gustaf Aulén made a typology of three classic models: Christus Victor, moral influence, and satisfaction. He rediscovered the earliest view, Christus Victor, and helped clarify how the three models are different from each other. Others have come along since and created variations or even new theories that springboard off one of the three classic views. Two of those hybrid models are narrative Christus Victor and penal substitutionary atonement. Finally, anthropologist René Girard connected the death of Jesus with the "scapegoat" tendency found in almost every human society.
3. Biblical writers, particularly Paul, understood evil to be not only personified but also a spiritual phenomenon. In cosmic terms, Paul talks about angels and spiritual elements. God originally created the powers as something good (Colossians 1:15-17). These structures were created as a network of norms and regularities by which civilization could be built and have order. But now they are fallen, wanting the allegiance of humanity instead of being servants to God and humanity. They strive to be God. Thus they are fallen and need to be redeemed. Some biblical scholars say that the powers killed Jesus. By refusing to react violently, Jesus disarmed the powers through his death and resurrection, unmasking them by making public spectacles of them (Colossians 2:13-15). His resurrection exposed the powers, revealing that they aren't the all-powerful entities they purport to be.
4. Anselm developed this model in his book *Cur Deus homo?*, often translated *Why Did God Become a Man?*
5. J. Denny Weaver, "The Nonviolent Atonement: Human Violence, Discipleship and God," in *Stricken by God? Nonviolent*

Identification and the Victory of Christ, ed. Brad Jersak and Michael Hardin (Grand Rapids, MI: Eerdmans Publishing), 316–37.

6 James H. Cone, *The Cross and the Lynching Tree* (Maryknoll, NY: Orbis Books, 2011), 161.

7 Some of those voices are Rita Nakashima Brock, "And a Little Child Will Lead Us: Christology and Child Abuse," in *Christianity, Patriarchy, and Abuse: A Feminist Critique*, ed. Joanne Carlson Brown and Carole R. Bohn (New York: Pilgrim Press, 1989), 50–54; and Delores S. Williams, *Sisters in the Wilderness: The Challenge of Womanist God-Talk* (Maryknoll, NY: Orbis Books, 1993), 161–67.

8 James Alison, "Some Thoughts on the Atonement," *James Alison* (blog), last modified July 30, 2006, http://www.jamesalison.co.uk/texts/eng11.html.

Chapter 5

1 Theologian Christopher Marshall writes: "In a real sense, the power to inflict violent death, and the capacity to evoke counter-violence from victims, is the most potent evidence of sin's grip over humanity. If sin is to be defeated, then, violence must be overcome once and for all. This is what Jesus sought to do. But to succeed in doing so, it was not enough simply to avoid inflicting violence on others, or to teach people to love their enemies. He also had to withstand the temptation to hit back; he had to break the cycle of violence and revenge, hatred and counter-hatred. He even had to endure violence himself—the supreme violence of an unjust execution—without seeking or desiring retaliation. He had to absorb the very worst that the powers could do, he had to go to the very limits of human desolation and at that point pray, 'Father, forgive them, for they do not know what they are doing' (Luke 23:34). In so doing Jesus deconstructed the power and logic of evil." Christopher Marshall, *All Things Reconciled: Essays on Restorative Justice, Religious Violence, and the Interpretation of Scripture* (Eugene, OR: Cascade Books, 2018), 182.

2 David Shenk, email to the author.

3 Mark D. Baker and Joel B. Green, *Recovering the Scandal of the Cross: Atonement in New Testament and Contemporary Contexts*, 2nd ed. (Downers Grove, IL: InterVarsity Press Academic, 2011), 192–205.

The Author

Michele Hershberger is the author of *God's Story, Our Story*; *A Christian View of Hospitality*; and several other books. She serves as chair of the Bible department at Hesston College, where she teaches Bible and youth ministry classes. With a degree from Anabaptist Mennonite Biblical Seminary, Hershberger has devoted her life to serving the church as pastor, writer, speaker, and instructor. She and her husband, Del Hershberger, have three children and are members of Hesston Mennonite Church.

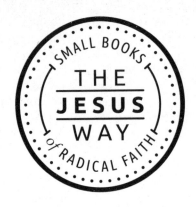

Small Books of the Jesus Way of Radical Faith

What Is the Bible and How Do We Understand It?
by Dennis R. Edwards

Why Did Jesus Die and What Difference Does It Make?
by Michele Hershberger

What Is God's Mission in the World and How Do We Join It?
by Juan F. Martínez
(SPRING 2020)

Why Do We Suffer and Where Is God When We Do?
by Valerie G. Rempel
(SPRING 2020)

What Is the Trinity and Why Does It Matter?
by Steve Dancause
(SUMMER 2020)

Who Are Our Enemies and How Do We Love Them?
by Hyung Jin Kim Sun
(SUMMER 2020)

What Is the Church and Why Does It Exist?
by David Fitch
(FALL 2020)

What Does Justice Look Like and Why Does God Care about It?
by Judith and Colin McCartney
(FALL 2020)

What Is God's Kingdom and What Does Citizenship Look Like?
by César García
(SPRING 2021)

Who Was Jesus and What Does It Mean to Follow Him?
by Nancy Elizabeth Bedford
(SPRING 2021)

Herald Press

www.HeraldPress.com. 1-800-245-7894